AT TWILIGHT:
A PLAY FOR TWO ACTORS, THREE MUSICIANS, ONE DANCER, EIGHT MASKS (AND A DONKEY COSTUME)

GRAHAM EATOUGH
& SIMON STARLING

LIST OF CHARACTERS

EEYORE
— from A.A. Milne's *Winnie-the-Pooh* stories

SIMON STARLING
— artist

GRAHAM EATOUGH
— theatre maker

WILLIAM BUTLER YEATS
— poet & playwright

EZRA POUND
— poet & translator

OLD MAN
— from Yeats' play *At the Hawk's Well*

YOUNG MAN
— from Yeats' play *At the Hawk's Well*

ROCK DRILL
— sculpture by Jacob Epstein (*spectre of World War I*)

NANCY CUNARD
— socialite and heiress

MICHIO ITO
— dancer

THE GUARDIAN OF THE WELL / THE HAWK*
— from Yeats' play *At the Hawk's Well*

Two actors, in various masks, play all the characters, including Simon Starling and Graham Eatough, for whom there are no masks.

*The Guardian of the Well hawk is played by a dancer.

LIST OF MASKS/COSTUMES

EEYORE

W.B. YEATS

EZRA POUND (AFTER HENRI GAUDIER-BRZESKA)

NANCY CUNARD (AFTER CONSTANTIN BRANCUSI)

MICHIO ITO (AFTER ISAMU NOGUCHI)

ROCK DRILL (AFTER JACOB EPSTEIN)

OLD MAN (AFTER EDMUND DULAC)

YOUNG MAN (AFTER EDMUND DULAC)

THE GUARDIAN OF THE WELL (AFTER EDMUND DULAC)

LIST OF PROPS

Hawk cloth

Nine blast trees

Lectern

Two fencing foils

TWILIGHT

A PROCESSION

In front of the audience is some staging, representing a Japanese Noh theatre, including a hashigakari, or bridge section, and a projection screen across the up-stage edge.

Once the audience has gathered, Eeyore, played by the two actors in the donkey costume, leads the musicians down the driveway, through the garden and into the performance space.

Eeyore separates to reveal Simon and Graham.

Gongs are rung to signal the start of the play.

AT THE HAWK'S WELL I

The musicians meet on the stage area, unfold the Hawk Cloth and show it to the audience. It is then folded up again and placed up-stage-centre in front of the screen to represent the well.

On the projection screen the hawk enters, covered in a cloak, and kneels in a position in front of the folded Hawk Cloth.

OVERTURE

Sung by the musicians:

> I call to the eye of the mind
> A well long choked up and dry
> And boughs long stripped by the wind,
> And I call to the mind's eye
> Pallor of an ivory face,
> Its lofty dissolute air,
> A man climbing up to a place
> The salt sea wind has swept bare.

Graham goes to get the Old and Young Man masks.
He gives the Old Man mask to Simon and directs him to his
entrance along the bridgeway.

Simon enters the stage wearing the mask of the Old Man.

He stands for a moment, motionless by the side of the stage with
bowed head. He lifts his head at the sound of a drum tap. He goes
towards the front of the stage moving to the taps of the drum. He
crouches and moves his hands as if making a fire. His movements,
like those of the other persons of the play, suggest a marionette.
The Old Man falls asleep.

Graham enters along the bridgeway wearing the mask
of the Young Man.

He moves towards the Old Man and wakes him.
The Old Man is startled and afraid. He moves towards the
back of the stage to protect the well.

MUSIC

SIMON: Good evening. My name is Simon Starling, I'm an artist.

Simon removes the Old Man mask, places it on a tree and moves to
the lectern at the front of the stage. Graham is still in his Young Man
mask and continuing with the Hawk's Well scene. A moment of
confusion as Graham realises Simon has stopped. Simon waits for
Graham to take off his mask and join him at the front of the stage.
Throughout the following, Graham is keen to return to the
performance.

SIMON: Good evening. My name is Simon Starling, I'm an artist.

GRAHAM: And I'm Graham Eatough, a theatre maker.

AT TWILIGHT

SIMON: And this is twilight. In Japanese culture, twilight or *higure* is neither darkness nor light, nor even a mixture of the two, more a grayness, the most suggestive colour in all Japanese art. It is a world of singularly subtle shades that exist solely in that momentary space of entering darkness from light, of entering night from day. The space between fiction and reality, the living and the dead.

GRAHAM: We're here to perform for you this evening W.B Yeats' play, *At the Hawk's Well*, the first part of which you've just been watching.

SIMON: Our setting is the grounds of Holmwood House, the Alexander "Greek" Thomson villa originally designed for the Couper family, owners of the paper mill on the River Cart below.

GRAHAM: (Interrupts) We hope you enjoy the rest of the performance

Graham makes to go up-stage and resume the Hawk's Well scene. Simon remains at the lectern. Graham realises, with some frustration, that Simon is not ready to continue with the scene.

SIMON: In 2010, while working on *Project for a Masquerade (Hiroshima)*, a 16th century Japanese Noh drama of personal reinvention, double identities and disguise, restaged as a Cold War drama, I unearthed the story of two poets similarly redeploying the modes and manners of Noh theatre to contemporary effect.

Graham moves around the stage to indicate its different elements whilst Simon remains at the lectern. Graham describes the different elements of the stage briskly, so as to get on with the performance.

SIMON: In the three winters of 1913-16, as the First World War raged on across the Channel, William Butler Yeats and Ezra Pound lived together at Stone Cottage, in the tranquil setting of Ashdown Forest in Sussex. It was here that the younger poet, Pound, introduced his mentor, Yeats, to the ancient art of Japanese Noh theatre and where they began work on a contemporary Noh drama, *At the Hawk's Well*.

GRAHAM: Our stage represents that of the Japanese Noh theatre. The *hashigakari*, or bridgeway, provides the main entrance to the Noh stage and a bridge between the actors and their characters, the past and the present, the living and the dead, the mortal and divine. The three musicians make up our Noh theatre's *hayashi* who accompany the play: Joshua Abrams, Lisa Alvarado, and Mikel Avery. Appropriately, ancient pine trees surround our stage. In Noh theatre the pine tree represents a ladder, or stairway, down which the gods can descend to the stage and the world of the living.

SIMON: Around our stage are positioned eight other trees, blast trees, that act in the different layers of our story. They represent the decimated landscape of the First World War, as well as the trees of Ashdown Forest. The trees also double as the faerie woods of Yeats' poetic imagination, steeped in the mythology of Celtic Ireland in the heroic age, and the setting for his own Noh-inspired drama, *At the Hawk's Well*.

GRAHAM: On these trees we have eight masks representing the central characters of our story; Ezra Pound...

AT TWILIGHT

Graham moves from character to character to introduce them, adopting Noh style poses and movements.

SIMON: Yeats' young colleague and secretary is spending this time in the bucolic Sussex countryside to complete a series of translations of ancient Japanese Noh plays. (A somewhat spurious process of monolingual translation carried out by someone with no knowledge of the Japanese language and based on the scattered fragments left by a dead man—Ernest Fenollosa.)

GRAHAM: W.B. Yeats…

SIMON: These plays, translated into English for the first time, offer the ageing Yeats an artistic way forward. He has become disillusioned with the modes and manners of contemporary European theatre (his involvement with the Abbey Theatre in Dublin being largely behind him) and these aristocratic Japanese Noh dramas, with their spare economy and shape-shifting characters, captivate him. Noh's symbolic bridgeway and pine tree, that act as transcendental portals to the spirit world, seem to rhyme with the poet's own interests in séances and spirituality.

Graham as the Young Man stamps three times.

SIMON: Against this backdrop of his adventures into the spirit world, Yeats writes *At the Hawk's Well*. The story tells of a young warrior, Cuchulain, from the Irish Golden Age, and his search for immortality at a magical well.

Graham as the Young Man goes to stand at the well.

SIMON: Also at the well is the Old Man who has wasted most of his life waiting for the magical water to appear.

Graham as the Young Man stands to look at The Guardian of the Well.

SIMON: The well is guarded by the mysterious hawk-like woman who wards off visitors.

GRAHAM: Nancy Cunard...

SIMON: The play was performed for the first time exactly one hundred years ago to a hand-picked audience at the Cavendish Square residence of the wealthy socialite, Lady Cunard.

GRAHAM: And Rock Drill...

SIMON: Jacob Epstein's sculpture was to become iconic of the Vorticists, the group of young artists led by Wyndham Lewis and Ezra Pound. This short-lived modernist movement, inspired by The Machine Age, saw its demise in the face of the unfolding catastrophe of the First World War.

Graham is becoming impatient. He has kept hold of the Pound mask but goes up-stage to contemplate the hawk.

SIMON: With *At the Hawk's Well*, Yeats created a hybrid drama somewhere between traditional Japanese Noh theatre, Irish mythology and contemporary chamber theatre. Its story seems to mimic the story of the two poets Yeats and Pound, at either ends of their careers, during their time together at Stone Cottage. Their ongoing search for literary immortality echoing the young Cuchulain's battle with the Old Man for the life-giving waters of the illusive well.

GRAHAM: I think that's pretty clear now Simon. It's all in the play.

SIMON: Well, it's actually a fairly complicated tale to tell. It may be interesting to know that the original Noh drama, *Yōrō*, on which *At the Hawk's Well* is based, is set in the time of the twenty-first Emperor, Yūryaku. The Emperor is told of a rumour about a miraculous spring in Motosu of Mino Province (present-day Gifu Prefecture) and dispatches an imperial investigator to find out about it. At the site, the investigator meets an old woodcutter and his son who had found the spiritual spring…

Simon is interrupted by Graham prodding him with the rapier.

THE FENCING LESSON I

Graham is wearing the Pound mask on the top of his head. He has picked up one of the rapiers and is prodding Simon into action with it.

GRAHAM: A fencing lesson—the younger and by nature more swashbuckling poet, Ezra Pound…

SIMON: the "Idaho kid", dressed in piratical clothing—earring, cape, big beret, loud colours…

GRAHAM: …teaches his elder and physically more awkward mentor and employer, W.B. Yeats, the art of swordplay.

Graham hands Simon the Yeats mask and the other rapier. Graham demonstrates, Simon copies.

GRAHAM /POUND: Your first move is to put on the mask. First put the lower part of the mask under your chin, and then

pull the top over your head, all with the left hand.
Never help yourself with the armed hand.

Graham helps Simon into the initial fencing pose (these actions also resonate with the ritualistic donning of the Noh mask and the assumption of character).

GRAHAM
/POUND: In keeping with chivalrous traditions, you always salute your opponent before crossing blades. Should there be judging officials or an audience, you salute them too. Look your adversary straight in the eye, bodily erect, foil down. Keeping the right elbow almost in contact with your body, bring the foil up pointing it straight at the ceiling, the blade in front of your right eye. Halt it there for a second or two: then, energetically sweep it down and away to the right of you. The blade must whistle through the air, and this sound is the opening bar of the symphony of fencing.

MUSIC

They enact a Noh-style fencing dance.

SIMON
/YEATS: (*Aside, raising mask*)
A few weeks ago Pound took a great distaste to another poet's work and sent him a challenge to meet him in France and fight a duel on the grounds that such poetry was an affront to the reader. The other poor man was deeply depressed for many days at the thought of being so disliked. I feel I have a very vigorous secretary. I am careful however to dictate my letters.

They fence some more. Yeats has to stop from tiredness.

SIMON
/YEATS: (*Recovering*)
I like to fence for half an hour at the day's end,
and when I close my eyes upon the pillow I see a
foil playing before me, the button to my face.
We meet always in the deep of the mind, whatever
our work, wherever our reverie carries us, that
other Will.

Simon takes off the Yeats mask and returns to the lectern.
Graham is still in the Pound mask, ready to continue.

SIMON
/YEATS: Ezra's mask is based on fellow vorticist, Henri
Gaudier-Brzeska's 1914 stone carving *Hieratic Head of Ezra Pound*. Now in Washington at the
National Gallery of Art, during World War I
this talismanic bust of the young poet was kept
in the garden of author and literary hostess Violet
Hunt, who maintained that Pound's presence,
at least his sculpted image, warded off German
Zeppelins. Every Monday Yeats travelled
from Ashdown Forest to London for a regular
appointment with his medium. It was during these
séances that he was contacted by the spirit of Leo
Africanus, a sixteenth century Moorish traveller
and scholar...

AT THE HAWK'S WELL 2

Graham retrieves the Young Man mask and adopts his position from
the end of At the Hawk's Well 1. He starts the next speech whilst
Simon is still at the lectern.

YOUNG MAN: You can, it may be,
Lead me to what I seek, a well wherein
Three hazels drop their nuts and withered leaves,
And where a solitary girl keeps watch

                    Among grey boulders. He who drinks, they say,
                    Of that miraculous water lives for ever.

OLD MAN: And are there not before your eyes at the instant
                    Grey boulders and a solitary girl
                    And three stripped hazels?

YOUNG MAN: But there is no well.

OLD MAN: Can you see nothing yonder?

YOUNG MAN: I but see
                    A hollow among stones half-full of leaves.

OLD MAN: And do you think so great a gift is found
                    By no more toil than spreading out a sail,
                    And climbing a steep hill? Oh, folly of youth,
                    Why should that hollow place fill up for you,
                    That will not fill for me? I have lain in wait
                    For more than fifty years, to find it empty,
                    Or but to find the stupid wind of the sea
                    Drive round the perishable leaves.

YOUNG MAN: So it seems
                    There is some moment when the water fills it.

OLD MAN: A secret moment that the holy shades
                    That dance upon the desolate mountain know,
                    And not a living man, and when it comes
                    The water has scarce plashed before it is gone.

YOUNG MAN: I will stand here and wait. Why should the luck
                    Of Sualtim's son desert him now? For never
                    Have I had long to wait for anything.

OLD MAN: No! Go from this accursed place. This place
                    Belongs to me, that girl there and those others,
                    Deceivers of men.

AT TWILIGHT

YOUNG MAN: And who are you who rail
Upon those dancers that all others bless?

OLD MAN: One whom the dancers cheat. I came like you
When young in body and in mind, and blown
By what had seemed to me a lucky sail.
The well was dry, I sat upon its edge,
I waited the miraculous flood, I waited
While the years passed and withered me away.
I have snared the birds for food and eaten grass
And drunk the rain, and neither in dark nor shine
Wandered too far away to have heard the plash,
And yet the dancers have deceived me. Thrice
I have awakened from a sudden sleep
To find the stones were wet.

YOUNG MAN: My luck is strong,
It will not leave me waiting, nor will they
That dance among the stones put me asleep;
If I grow drowsy I can pierce my foot.

OLD MAN: No, do not pierce it, for the foot is tender,
It feels pain much. But find your sail again
And leave the well to me, for it belongs
To all that's old and withered.

YOUNG MAN: No, I stay.

MUSIC

The cry of the hawk.

YOUNG MAN: There is that bird again.

OLD MAN: There is no bird.

YOUNG MAN: It sounded like the sudden cry of a hawk,

But there's no wing in sight. As I came hither
A great grey hawk swept down out of the sky,
And though I have good hawks,
the best in the world
I had fancied, I have not seen its like. It flew
As though it would have torn me with its beak,
Or blinded me, smiting with that great wing.
I had to draw my sword to drive it off,
And after that it flew from rock to rock.
I pelted it with stones, a good half-hour,
And just before I had turned the big rock there
And seen this place, it seemed to vanish away.
Could I but find a means to bring it down
I'd hood it.

OLD MAN: The Woman of the Sidhe herself,
The mountain witch, the unappeasable shadow,
She is always flitting upon this mountain-side,
To allure or to destroy. When she has shown
Herself to the fierce women of the hills
Under that shape they offer sacrifice
And arm for battle. There falls a curse
On all who have gazed in her unmoistened eyes;
So get you gone while you have that proud step
And confident voice, for not a man alive
Has so much luck that he can play with it.
Those that have long to live should fear her most,
The old are cursed already. That curse may be
Never to win a woman's love and keep it;
Or always to mix hatred in the love;
Or it may be that she will kill your children,
That you will find them, their throats torn
and bloody,
Or you will be so maddened that you kill them
With your own hand.

Graham as Young Man moves towards the hawk. Simon takes off the Old Man mask and moves back down towards the lectern. Graham continues as Young Man.

AT TWILIGHT

YOUNG MAN: Have you been set down there
To threaten all who come, and scare them off?
You seem as dried up as the leaves and sticks,
As though you had no part in life.

Another hawk cry.

Simon continues with the lecture.

SÉANCES

SIMON: Every Monday Yeats travelled from Ashdown Forest to London for a regular appointment with his medium. It was during these séances that he was contacted by the spirit of Leo Africanus, a sixteenth century Moorish traveller and scholar, who Yeats came to regard as his spiritual alter-ego or "anti-self". Leo was self-assured and impulsive, all that his name and Africa might suggest, whilst Yeats was cautious and timid.

Graham has taken off the Young Man mask and reluctantly returned down-stage to join Simon.

GRAHAM: Back at Stone Cottage, Yeats began a correspondence with the spirit of Leo Africanus in which he would write to and 'from' the dead man, allowing him to control his thoughts. These letters were part of Yeats' meditations on *The Doctrine of the Mask* in which Yeats explored the idea that every passionate man is linked with another age in which he might find an opposite that could complete him. This was the same confrontation between the living and the dead, this world and the next, that Yeats and Pound were exploring in the twilight world of the Noh plays.

SIMON: For Yeats, Pound was also a "spiritual anti-self": young, vital, flamboyant. In his letters to Leo Africanus and his relationship with Pound, Yeats was confronting his opposite in both heaven and earth.

Graham has retrieved the Yeats and Pound masks. Yeats and Pound return to fencing–their sport accompanied by the dictation of a letter, and interrupted by their verbal duelling.

SIMON
/YEATS: Take a letter Mr. Pound.

My Dear Mabel, I came down here yesterday and so being in the hurry of change could not write to you. I shall be here for a couple of months returning to London every Monday and staying until Tuesday so that I may visit my friends. Ezra Pound and his wife are staying with me and are to read to me when artificial light makes my eyes useless–it is a problem what I do with my eyes every winter. Ezra has a charming young wife who looks as if her face was made of Dresden china.

(Aside)
I look at her in perpetual wonder. It is hard to believe she is real!

(Mask up on his head)
Yet she spends all her daylight hours making the most monstrous cubist pictures.

GRAHAM
/POUND: My wife had an amusing dream about me a few nights ago. I was hanging to the top of a very straight pine tree-all-stem-&-a-burst-of-branches-at-the-top-kind. I had not climbed it—she said I'd got there by translation.

SIMON
/YEATS: And I thought your powers of translation
            remained purely linguistic?

*They fence some more. The fencing becomes increasingly serious
and energetic. Both men seem to be straining to defeat the other.
Pound eventually forces Yeats, with some violence, into submission
during the next speech.*

SIMON
/YEATS: Sometimes when you are dreaming you will
            imagine that you witness or take part in a dispute.
            And afterwards, when you examine the opinions,
            discover that both disputants have made use
            of thoughts that are a part of your daily mind.
            Whose was that other that opposed you? And
            when you lie in bed after fencing you see, for
            certain minutes, a foil darting upon you from the
            darkness and whirling its point hither and thither.
            What hand holds the point upon you?

*They dust themselves down making light of the fight and
return to the business of letter dictation*

SIMON
/YEATS: The play goes on well except for Ainley who waves
            his arms like a drowning kitten and the musician
            who is in a constant rage. (*Musicians interject.*)
            I went to Dulac's on Tuesday and saw the mask
            that he has made for Cuchulain, a Greek head and
            helmet with the look of something older, perhaps
            Egyptian? The masks have the most wonderful
            effect. They keep their power when you're quite
            close. The form is a discovery and the dancing and
            the masks wonderful. I believe I have at last found
            a dramatic form that suits me.
            Yours etc...

GRAHAM
/POUND: (*Aside*)
            Yeats' play must go on… I have some undefined
            marginal function which mostly consists of
            watching W.B. rushing about a studio shouting
            'Now…NOW…Now…Now you really must…'
            etc… I am a TIGER when I get to rehearsing.
            We rehearsed at Lady Cunard's.

Graham lifts the Pound mask from his head and moves over to the Nancy Cunard mask.

NANCY CUNARD

GRAHAM: Ezra Pound first met Nancy Cunard at her
            mother's home in Cavendish Square as Pound was
            making preparations for the performance of *At
            the Hawk's Well*. Nancy is represented here in the
            abstracted form of Constantin Brancusi's polished
            bronze *Portrait of Nancy Cunard (*or *Sophisticated
            Young Lady)*. She was astonishingly beautiful; she
            had an elegant demeanour regardless of what she
            was wearing or where she was wearing it. She was
            very tall and very slim with a graceful sway in her
            walk that was like a delicate dance.

Graham puts on the mask and becomes Nancy.

MUSIC

NANCY'S DANCE

SIMON: Nancy, whose capacity for alcohol and affairs
            became legendary, felt the need to dress in
            disguise when she went out, to wear costumes
            of her own making. Once she was arrested for
            swimming at dawn in the Serpentine, emerging

before the authorities drenched in a homemade outfit of velvet, chiffon, ribbons, feathers, spangles and artificial flowers.

From the beginning Nancy found Pound physically appealing: his thick wavy red hair, pointed beard, and lynx green eyes.

Graham, still as Nancy, has picked up the Pound mask and starts to dance with it, holding it in front of him.

GRAHAM
/NANCY: So striking behind his pince-nez. There was a good deal of panache to him, a certain flamboyance. His learned blasts might alarm but he was vibrating and dynamic and he could certainly become ecstatic!

Graham is wearing the Nancy mask while tenderly holding the Pound mask over his shoulder.

THE DANCE OF NANCY AND POUND

(Music stops momentarily)

GRAHAM
/POUND: Behold what perils do environ
The man who meddles with a siren.

Graham eventually removes the Nancy mask and lays it on the floor. Still wearing the Pound mask, he kneels besides Nancy.

GRAHAM: Later, when she became critically ill, Pound remained at her side, and their long love affair began. Their correspondence exposes a woman who wanted him passionately and, when rejected, stood by him, as so many of the women who loved him did.

MICHIO ITO

SIMON: *(Still at the lectern. Introducing the Ito mask)* "The Famous Male Dancer Michio Ito Who has Created a Furore in Society with his Repertoire of Harmonized Europo-Japanese Dances."

GRAHAM: It wasn't until Japanese dancer Michio Ito's appearance on the London scene that Yeats could conceive of how to stage a Noh play of his own.

Simon pulls down the Yeats mask over his face

Yeats: I saw him as the tragic image that stirred my imagination. As he rose from the floor, where he had been sitting cross-legged, or as he threw out an arm, he was able to recede from us into some more powerful life.

GRAHAM: Ito had seen Noh as a child but was frankly more interested in the European new wave of dance by the Ballets Russes and Nijinsky that he'd been inspired by during his recent time in Paris and Berlin.

Graham tries on the Ito mask.

GRAHAM/ITO: As far as I am concerned there is nothing more boring than Noh.

Simon pulls up the Yeats mask

SIMON: But Ito arrived in London penniless and in dire need of any gainful employment. After performing his hybrid dances in the salons of the wealthy, he was approached by Yeats and Pound and persuaded of the value of Japanese drama.

THE ZOO

Graham as Ito approaches the hawk's mask and begins to rehearse the movements of the bird. These movements prefigure the final 'turning' section of the hawk's dance from the end of the play.

Simon is wearing the Yeats mask on the back of his head and turns this to face the audience at points during the next speech, creating a little "turning" dance of his own and echoing Graham/Ito's movements up-stage.

SIMON: There is a story that Ito danced outside the hawk's cage at London Zoo, prancing, swirling, gyrating and flapping his arms in imitation of the bird, as Yeats stood by encouragingly. While a crowd gathered to see the "madman". According to some, Yeats also danced before the amazed populace. I cannot vouch for Michio Ito, but so far as Yeats is concerned the story must be branded not only apocryphal but also utterly improbable.

Graham ends his rehearsal as Ito by making the hawk's cry, which is represented in the music. He repeats this cry, which continues to be echoed in the music, as he moves up-stage, directing it towards Simon as a way of goading him into action. He collects the Yeats and Pound masks in readiness for the next section.

AT THE HAWK'S WELL 3

Graham and Simon put on the Old Man and Young Man masks and adopt the positions from the end of At the Hawk's Well 2. We hear the hawk's cry again in the music.

YOUNG MAN: That cry!
There is that cry again. That woman made it,
But why does she cry out as the hawk cries?

OLD MAN: It was her mouth, and yet not she, that cried.
It was that shadow cried behind her mouth;
And now I know why she has been so stupid
All the day through, and had such heavy eyes.
Look at her shivering now, the terrible life
Is slipping through her veins. She is possessed.
Who knows whom she will murder or betray
Before she awakes in ignorance of it all,
And gathers up the leaves? But they'll be wet;
The water will have come and gone again;
That shivering is the sign. Oh, get you gone,
At any moment now I shall hear it bubble.
If you are good you will leave it. I am old,
And if I do not drink it now, will never;
I have been watching all my life and maybe
Only a little cupful will bubble up.

YOUNG MAN: I'll take it in my hands. We shall both drink,
And even if there are but a few drops,
Share them.

On the screen The Guardian of the Well throws off her cloak and rises. Her dress under the cloak suggests a hawk.

OLD MAN: But swear that I may drink the first;
The young are greedy, and if you drink the first
You'll drink it all. Ah, you have looked at her;
She has felt your gaze and turned her eyes on us;
I cannot bear her eyes, they are not of this world,
Nor moist, nor faltering; they are no girl's eyes.

The Old Man covers his head to protect himself from the hawk's gaze. The hawk's dance has begun on screen.

YOUNG MAN: Why do you gaze upon me with the eyes
of a hawk?
I am not afraid of you, bird, woman, or witch.

AT TWILIGHT

The Young Man goes to the side of the well, which the Guardian of the Well has left.

YOUNG MAN: Do what you will, I shall not leave this place
Till I have grown immortal like yourself.

He has sat down, the Girl has begun to dance, moving like a hawk. The Old Man sleeps. The dance continues.

The dance continues. The Young Man rises slowly.

MUSICIAN: The madness has laid hold upon him now,
For he grows pale and staggers to his feet.

The dance has reached the final "turning" section.

YOUNG MAN: Run where you will,
Grey bird, you shall be perched upon my wrist,
Some were called queens and yet have been perched there.

MUSICIAN: (*Speaking*)
I have heard water plash; it comes, it comes;
It glitters among the stones and he has heard the plash; Look, he has turned his head.

The hawk has gone out. The Young Man follows, as if in a dream.

MUSICIAN: (*Singing*)
He has lost what may not be found
Till men heap his burial mound
And all the history ends.
He might have lived at his ease,
An old dog's head on his knees,
Among his children and friends.

The Old Man creeps up to the well.

OLD MAN: The accursed shadows have deluded me,
The stones are dark and yet the well is empty;
The water flowed and emptied while I slept,
You have deluded me my whole life through.
Accursed dancers, you have stolen my life.
That there should be such evil in a shadow!

Graham comes back on to join Simon/Old Man up-stage. Graham gives Simon/Old Man a consoling embrace and helps him off with his mask.

Graham goes to get the masks for Nancy and Rock Drill which are used as the fencing masks during the next section.

FENCING LESSON – REPRISE

GRAHAM: The First World War practically sounded the death knell of duelling. After its carnage, people realised that death needed some sort of holiday. After having braved the storms of fire and steel on the battlefield, few were willing to gamble their lives on the ground, quite possibly through the hands of a former friend. The duels that still occurred were almost bloodless affairs.

Graham and Simon stop fencing and lift their masks as they move to the front of the stage regaining their breath after the exercise. They continue to use the voices of Yeats and Pound for the following lines.

SIMON
/YEATS: I find I can keep the thought of war away from me and go on with my work.

GRAHAM
/POUND: Even with a whole battery of artillery deployed for our benefit on the heath before Stone Cottage?

Percussive music begins.

AT TWILIGHT

SIMON
/YEATS: That is as near as we'll get to the war zone
         I reckon.

WORLD WAR I

Graham puts the Rock Drill mask back on and moves to its tree where he assumes a pose reminiscent of the Epstein sculpture.

SIMON: Even though Jacob Epstein had been sufficiently affected by war's horror to invest his vorticist driller, from its very conception, with a pervasive sense of anxiety, by 1916 *The Rock Drill*, was withdrawn and dismantled. Epstein claimed to have lost interest in machinery, but it is likely that the escalating bloodshed in Europe influenced his decision. Too many close friends of Epstein and Pound had been slaughtered, including Henri Gaudier-Brzeska, and violence was no longer an impulse to be celebrated.

Graham has placed the (Gaudier-Brzeska-designed) Pound mask in front of him. So the following is staged as Rock Drill as Brzeska talking to Pound.

POUND: "Dear Ezra.
         Our woods are magnificent. I am just now quartered in trenches in the middle of them, they are covered with lily of the valley, it grows and flowers on the trench itself. In the night we have many nightingales to keep us company.
         They sing very finely and the loud noise of the usual attacks and counter-attacks does not disturb them in the least. It is very warm and nice out of doors, one does not mind sleeping on the ground now. We have the finest futurist music Marinetti can dream of, big guns, small guns, bomb-

throwers' reports, with a great difference between the German and the French, the different kinds of whistling from the shells, their explosion, the echo in the woods of the rifle fires, some short, discreet, others long, rolling, etc.; but it is all a stupid vulgarity, and I prefer the fresh wind in the leaves with a few songs from the birds.

What are you writing? Is there anything important or interesting going on in the world? I mean the 'artistic London'. I have read nothing, a desert in the head a very inviting place for a boche bullet or a shell. The Germans are restless, machine-gun crackling ahead, so I must end this in haste.

Yours ever,
Henri Gaudier-Brzeska

P.S. I have made an experiment. Two days ago I pinched from an enemy a mauser rifle. Its heavy unwieldy shape swamped me with a powerful image of brutality. I found that I did not like it. I broke the butt off and with my knife I carved in it a design, through which I tried to express a gentler order of feeling, which I preferred."

Graham takes off the Rock Drill mask and moves out of the sculpture position. He picks up the Pound mask and inspects it through the next speech before putting it back on.

GRAHAM
/POUND: He was killed at Neuville-Saint-Vaast, early this month, but the news is just in. This is the heaviest loss in personnel the arts have suffered by the war, it is not the case of a beautiful youth who had perhaps done his best work. Brzeska was five years younger than Brooke, but he was a man full

of vigorous genius, and there is no one to replace him. There is probably no artist fighting with any of the armies who might not have been better spared.

Graham/Pound joins Simon/Yeats at the front of the stage.
They face each other.

SIMON
/YEATS: I think it better that at times like these
We poets keep our mouths shut, for in truth
We have no gift to set a statesman right.

Graham has taken off the Pound mask and hands it to Simon.
Simon hands Graham the Yeats mask in return.
They put on each other's masks.

GRAHAM
/YEATS: He's had enough of meddling who can please
A young girl in the indolence of her youth
Or an old man upon a winter's night.

With the Pound mask still on the top of his head Graham moves away and begins to put on the back half of the Eeyore costume.
Simon returns to the lectern.

SIMON: This rare moment of cross-cultural, intergenerational collaboration was short lived. In the years after their time together at Stone Cottage Yeats' "stimulating yet irritating" young colleague and sparring partner became increasingly self absorbed, dismissive of his mentor's talents, and indeed disillusioned with Japanese theatre.

Graham with Pound mask (before dressing as Eeyore):

"I find Noh unsatisfactory … I admit there are beautiful bits in it. But it's all too damn soft."

SIMON: For his part Yeats continued to develop his Noh inspired dramas. Completed on his own deathbed in 1939, *The Death of Cuchulain*, the last in Yeats' cycle of 5 plays begun in 1916 with *At the Hawk's Well*, culminates with his dying hero tied to a pillar-stone. A bird comes and settles on his shoulder, and then with a shape-shifting transformation, carries off Cuchulain's spirit. Yeats' hawk, Michio Ito, left England for the United States in 1916 to forge a successful career as a dancer and choreographer. At the outbreak of World War II Ito, who had many influential friends and relatives in Japan, was wrongly accused of espionage and imprisoned. Following his return to Japan in 1943 as part of a prisoner exchange programme, Ito translated and restaged *At the Hawk's Well* for a Japanese audience. This time however Ito played the part of the Old Man. It should also be noted that today, bringing the process of appropriation and translation full circle, Tokyo based Noh master Umewaka Rokuro Gensho, is currently developing a deeply traditional Noh reinterpretation of Yeats' 1916 hybrid drama.

Simon is interrupted by Graham holding the front half of the Eeyore costume—he steps into it reluctantly while Graham continues at the lectern.

Graham and Simon look at each other. Simon puts on the head of the Eeyore costume and moves to the centre of the stage.

AT TWILIGHT

GRAHAM: The trees of Ashdown Forest that surround Stone Cottage were to be immortalised in Ernest Shepard's illustrations for A.A. Milne's *Winnie-the-Pooh* books after the war. Milne based Pooh's Hundred Acre Wood on Ashdown Forest where he lived and where, at the time Yeats and Pound were there, he was writing wartime propaganda articles for the Military Intelligence Department, MI7(b). Perhaps in reparation for this, in 1926 he wrote a denunciation of war titled *Peace with Honour*, only to retract this pacifist position again in the 1940s with his book *War with Honour*.

SIMON: 'Eeyore's Tail'

GRAHAM: 'In which Eeyore loses a tail and Pooh finds one.'

Graham/Pooh approaches Eeyore.

SIMON
/EEYORE: (*In a gloomy manner*)
How do you do?

GRAHAM
/POOH: And how are you?

Eeyore shakes his head from side to side.

EEYORE: Not very how. I don't seem to have felt at all how for a very long time.

POOH: Dear, dear. I'm sorry about that.
Let's have a look at you.

Eeyore stands, gazing sadly at the ground. Pooh walks all around him.

POOH: Why, what's happened to your tail?

EEYORE: What has happened to it?

POOH: It isn't there.

EEYORE: Are you sure?

POOH: Well, either a tail is there or it isn't there. You can't make a mistake about it. And yours isn't there!

EEYORE: Then what is?

POOH: Nothing.

EEYORE: Let's have a look.

Eeyore turns slowly around to the place where his tail had been a little while ago, and then, finding that he couldn't catch it up, he turned round the other way, until he comes back to where he was at first, and then he puts his head down and looks between his front legs.

EEYORE: (*With a sigh*)
I believe you're right.

POOH: Of course I'm right.

EEYORE: That accounts for a good deal. It explains everything. No wonder.

POOH: You must have left it somewhere.

EEYORE: Somebody must have taken it.
How like them.

Pause

POOH: Eeyore, I, Winnie-the-Pooh, will find your tail for you.

EEYORE: Thank you, Pooh. You're a real friend. Not like some.

Pooh goes off to look for Eeyore's tail.
He eventually finds it hanging from a tree.
He attaches it to the back of his costume.

Pooh approaches Eeyore and shows him the tail. Eeyore is delighted. Simon and Graham join together the two halves of the Eeyore costume and Eeyore is reunited with his tail. He frisks about the forest waving his tail happily.

Musicians sing:

> Who found the tail?
> I, said Pooh,
> At quarter to two
> (Only it was quarter to eleven really)
> I found the tail!

THE END

fig. 1

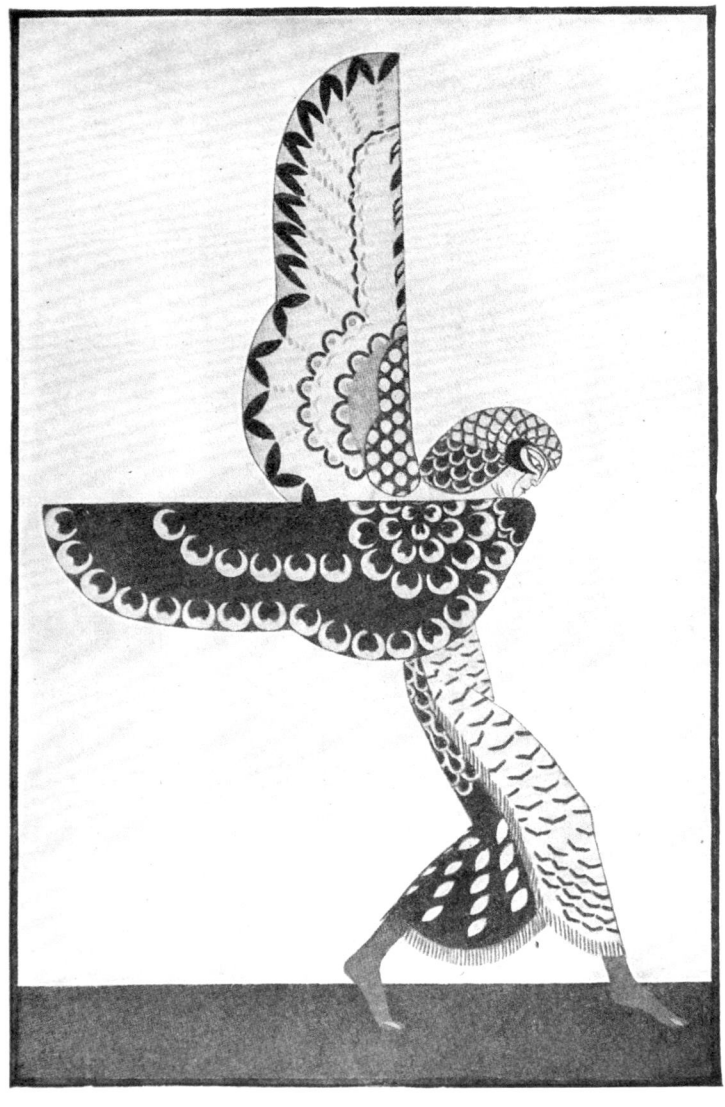

fig. 2

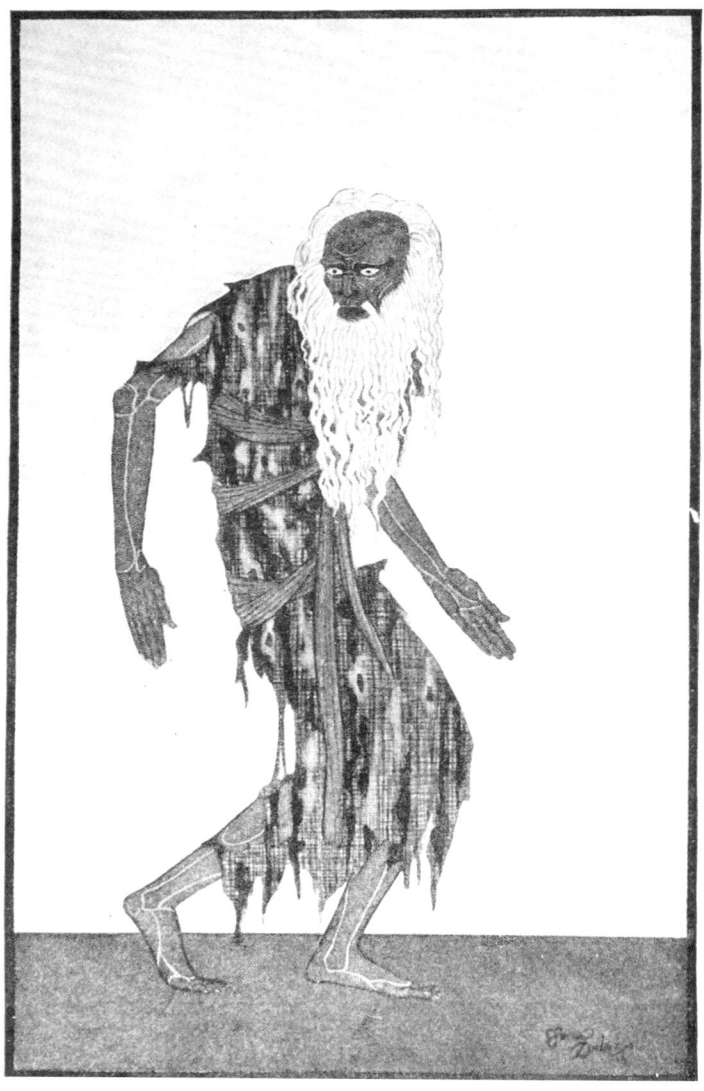

Katrina Brown, Director, The Common Guild

AT TWILIGHT
collaboration
and
performance

Twilight, that period between day and night, is said in Japanese culture to open up a portal to the spirit world, a potential moment of encounter with the past. It is a fitting context then for Simon Starling, who in his work has so often made use of the past to speak to the present. His previous works have been full of anachronisms, people and things displaced from one time to another, operating like a time machine cued up by objects. The aspirations and innovations of Modernism have long been a particular source of interest for Starling, along with the effects they brought about, including social and economic change. In this instance, the moment is one of extreme turmoil in Europe, in the throes of the First World War, and the "object", a play made by one of the most important European literary figures of the modern age: W.B. Yeats.

   Though Starling's work undoubtedly incorporates a kind of story-telling, it is one that suggest maps rather than linear narratives, and until now had not been manifest in live performances. Artists can, of course, be said to perform all the time: in talks or lectures, whether through the dialogue of the "in-conversation" event or the monologue of the lecture. Actual theatre began, however, to draw his interest when working in Japan, where he first encountered the highly stylised forms of Japanese Noh theatre, especially its use of masks. Noh made its first appearance in his work in *Project for a Masquerade (Hiroshima)* in 2010 [1], and a year later he developed a first scripted drama with a puppet theatre piece, *The Expedition*, a play in which a surrogate Starling appears as a marionette. These connected developments—coupled with his discovery of circumstances surrounding the coming into being of a Noh-inspired play by Yeats, *At the Hawk's Well* in 1916—made a tentative, curious step towards realising a live performance almost inevitable and set the process in motion for what was to become *At Twilight*.

      The project developed through collaboration with theatre director Graham Eatough, and was imagined as a new play, while also taking the form of an exhibition, that would include a group of new masks made by Yasuo Miichi in Osaka. Starling had first worked with Miichi on his *Project for a Masquerade (Hiroshima)*, which had suggested a piece of theatre that was, however, never developed. *At Twilight* developed into both a group of sculptures to be used in, and a script for, the new play, to be performed by two actors, presenting themselves initially as Starling and Eatough and, through the use of the masks and costumes, adopting the guise of several other characters.

      Extending from the core of the 1916 play through the circumstances of its coming into being, *At Twilight* weaves together some surprising and significant interconnections of influential figures and works through a particular time and place, a selection of which appear in the

---

[1]. "*Project for a Masquerade (Hiroshima)* was made for the Hiroshima City Museum of Contemporary Art and takes the form of a set of nine masks and a film. The work, which is ultimately a proposition for a piece of theatre, collapses the story of a 16th century Japanese Noh play, Eboshi-ori, onto the story surrounding the creation of 'Nuclear Energy', a monument to the beginnings of the atom bomb project, the so called 'Manhattan project', by the British sculptor Henry Moore. Each of the masks is a kind of hybrid object that fuses traditional Japanese forms with Western portraiture and caricature — each mask representing a historical or fictional character connected to the Cold War saga surrounding Moore's sculpture. The film was shot in the mask maker's studio in Osaka and charts the evolution of the masks from blocks of wood to fully formed characters and combines this visual narrative with the narratives of the Noh play and the sculpture." Simon Starling in interview with Pernille Albrethsen, 'Ten Questions – Simon Starling', *Kunstkritikk*, 2011

fig. 3

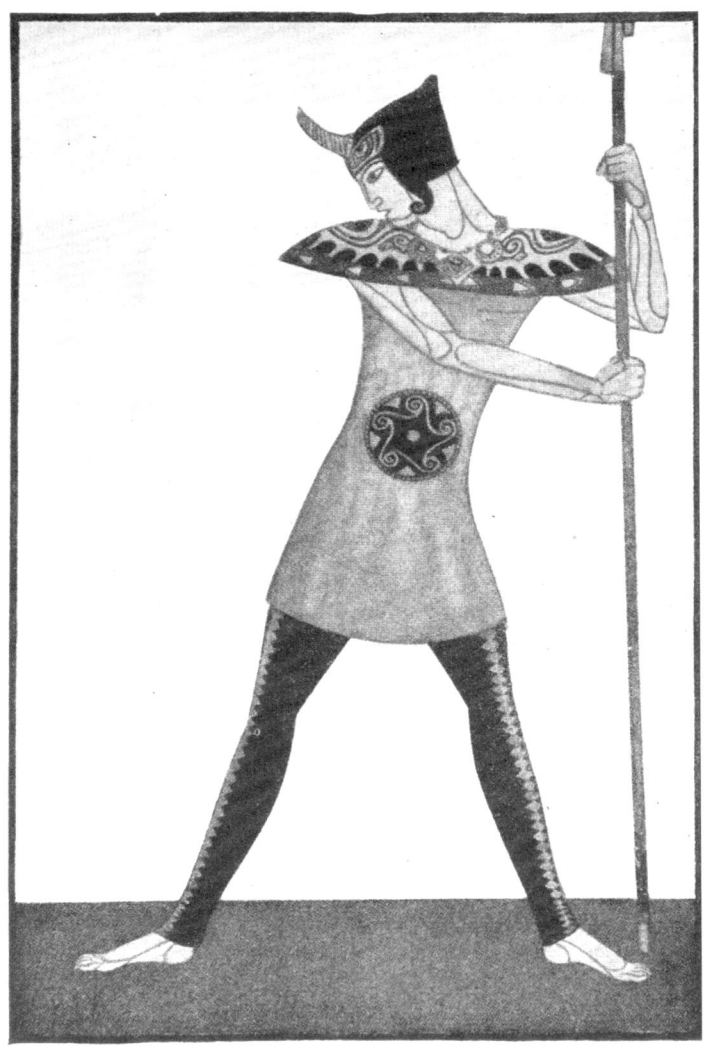

exhibition at the Japan Society in New York. *At the Hawk's Well* came to life in London during the First World War, in what Starling has described as "an odd cross-cultural mash-up in an English garden, at a traumatic moment in European history". The play was written by Yeats towards the end of a three-year period in which he was working with the considerably younger, American poet Ezra Pound (who was notionally functioning as Yeats' secretary [2]) and was inspired by a usefully scant awareness of traditional Noh theatre, to which Pound introduced him. Useful in that it allowed him to adopt those elements he was interested in, unconstrained by reverence to the considerable tradition. There is no doubt that had Yeats fully understood Noh, its meanings and conventions, or its intricacies, he would not and could not have made the play he did: it is based on partial knowledge, a superficial familiarity, co-opted in the spirit of innovation and experimentation. A good example of a little knowledge being "perhaps more potent" than in-depth knowledge. Yeats' play, written in verse, is a fusion of Irish folklore—the story of an old man in search of eternal life from an enchanted well and a young warrior, Cuchulain—and what he then saw as an exciting new possible form for theatre. It is highly stylised and symbolic and features only three characters, accompanied by three musicians and—representing the hawk of the title—a dancer.

      Eatough likens the process he and Starling embarked upon to an echo of Yeats' work in adapting an earlier Japanese drama *Yōrō* in that what they set about doing was "staging Yeats and Pound's staging, exposing those different layers of adaptation and production. You have these two actors playing Simon and me—they are our masks in a way, just as there are masks for all these other characters." [3]

2. For more on this see Longenbach, James: *Stone Cottage. Pound, Yeats & Modernism* Oxford and New York: Oxford University Press. (1988)

3. Quotes throughout from Eatough and Starling are, unless otherwise stated, drawn from a video interview at The Common Guild, Glasgow, on 1 July 2016

The fusion of ancient and modern that Yeats developed is also mirrored in *At Twilight* for it encapsulates a discourse between tradition and the avant-garde, between convention and something other, creating an absurd, dramatised tussle between history, mythology and Modernism.

It began with an attempt to consider a staging of the existent play, a work that came about in London as the result of shared interests, fragments of information, partial understandings, what would now be called "hybridisation". The creative process was—then and now—dependent on sharing, testing, debate, but crucially, that partial knowledge and understanding.

The crew of collaborators in 1916 extended beyond the two writers to include several others all coinciding in London: a French illustrator turned costume designer, Edmund Dulac (1882–1953); a Japanese dancer, Michio Ito (1892–1961); experimental photographer Alvin Langdon Coburn (1882–1966), whose photographs of the performers in costume are the only documents of the 1916 show; and Nancy Cunard (1896–1965), daughter of an heir to the Cunard Line shipping company and hostess for the performance. Starling has explained that, "the key players in the staging of this masquerade (both on stage and off) seem to have been striving to reinvent themselves by momentarily co-opting Oriental culture into a radically new Occidental moment—European Modernism." They each went on to become cemented in cultural history, something evidenced by the prism through which the appear in *At Twilight*, via portraits by leading photographers and sculptors.

This group is replicated in the current project by the multiple individuals involved. Starling approached Chicago-based musician Joshua Abrams and Natural Information

Society to make a new score to accompany the performance, having worked with Abrams on music for his *El Eco* project in Mexico City in 2015; and Venezuelan choreographer Javier De Frutos, working with Scottish Ballet, to devise a new danced segment to bring the Hawk to life, for *At Twilight* is, as its sub-title states, *A play for two actors, three musicians, one dancer, eight masks (and a donkey costume).* Working from and with 100-year old fragments, both Abrams and de Frutos set about creating something new, a process de Frutos described as "a 'who dunnit' I couldn't say no to". He worked with dancer Thomas Edwards and Abrams's music, as well as the hawk costume, made by Kumi Sakurai with Atelier Hinode in Tokyo, for Starling in 2014[4] based on Dulac's drawings and Coburn's photographs (greyscale, because of course no record survives of its colouring).

This monochrome palette continues in the blast trees that Starling made to support the masks. These figure-like stands made of charred wood are a direct reference to the ravaged landscapes of northern France, and the horrors that were unfolding through the First World War at the time. The impact of the war was far from remote: sculptor Henri Gaudier-Brzeska, on whose portrait of Pound Starling's mask is based, was killed in the trenches in 1915. In April 1916, Yeats was also deeply affected by the Easter Rising in Ireland[5]. That even in the midst of such catastrophe and horror, the avant-garde should be at work in pursuit of new forms is all the more remarkable.

The very place in which Yeats and Pound were at

4. The Hawk costume was made as part of Starling's installation for the 2014 Yokohama Triennale, along with similarly greyscale versions of the costumes for the other two characters in Yeats' play—the Old Man and the Young Man. The work is titled *At the Hawk's Well (Grayscale) Three costumes designed by Edmund Dulac and Michio Ito for the 1916 London premier of W.B. Yeats* Noh-inspired play for dancers, *At the Hawk's Well*, reproduced in a grayscale palette using available historical documentation'.

5. The Easter Rising against British rule in Ireland, which resulted in the execution of many of the Republican leaders, took place the same month as the performance of *At The Hawk's Well*, on 24 April 1916. Yeats wrote a poem *Easter, 1916* at the time, published in 1921, that included the oft-quoted, prophetic line, "a terrible beauty is born".

work in the winters of 1913—16 (although they also took time to fence)—Ashdown Forest in Sussex—gave rise to another significant cultural figure, and leads to perhaps the most unlikely character in *At Twilight*: Winnie-the-Pooh's famously gloomy donkey friend, Eeyore. For the forest was to become, ten years later, the inspiration for A.A.Milne's One Hundred Acre Wood. Eeyore appears in *At Twilight* as a two-part donkey costume, also made by Kumi Sakurai, based on multiple drawings. Eeyore, who is a poet in his own right, is brought to life in the play when inhabited by the two actors/Starling and Eatough/Pound and Yeats, a metaphor for the at times strained relationship between the two poets, that also adds a note of the absurd and a suggestion of that great British theatrical form: pantomime.

      The work that results from the process of collaboration over three years is, in Starling's words, "a piece of theatre made by a theatre director and an artist, which flips from being traditional theatre into something more approximating an artist's talk. It has elements of both of our worlds." It exists as both art and performance, the masks and costumes having a dual life as artworks and props, but is resolutely not the performance art of old that eschewed the attributes of theatre. It includes script, costumes, characters, lighting: all the very elements cast aside by the anti-theatrical impulse that characterised earlier live art. It contains extracts from the original play, draws on letters and notes made by some of those involved but adds a new layer, a tussle between the desire to act and the process of telling.

      Writing recently in *frieze*, about "why theatre remains vital", Lynne Tillman summarised:

> A play is words, also intensely physical, with actual bodies in space, and a viewer must watch and listen hard. A play foregrounds thinking. Words cause other words to come, and actions happen. Thinking

is present as an activity, and spoken and unspoken thoughts make up the play.[6]

At Twilight undoubtedly exposes thinking, but it is a play cloaked in images: of the black, blasted landscapes of northern France, of the Machine age future envisaged by the Vorticists. These are all present, captured in Starling's collage, a kind of "mind map" of the whole with the blackened tree at its core. *At Twilight* is in contemporary terms a "cross-cultural mash-up" but it is also a time-machine. It opens up a moment, a portal perhaps to 1916, but also remains resolutely grounded in its present and in the collaborative venture between artist and playwright, as well as musician, choreographer, costume-maker… a story-telling enterprise.

---

6. Lynne Tillman 'Play for Time' in *frieze*, no. 175, Nov – Dec 2015

fig. 4

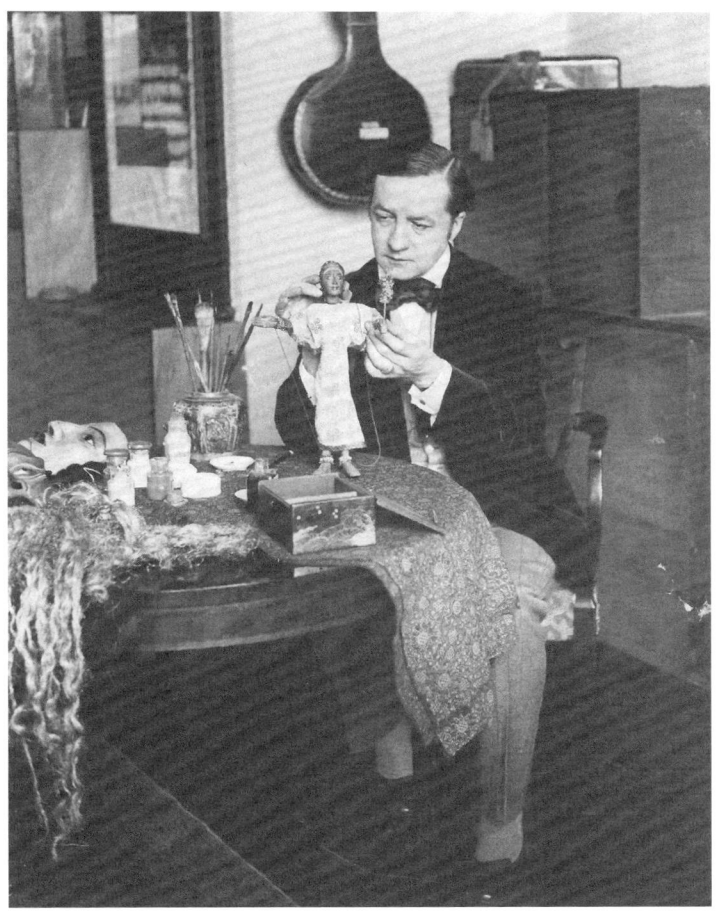

fig. 5 & 6

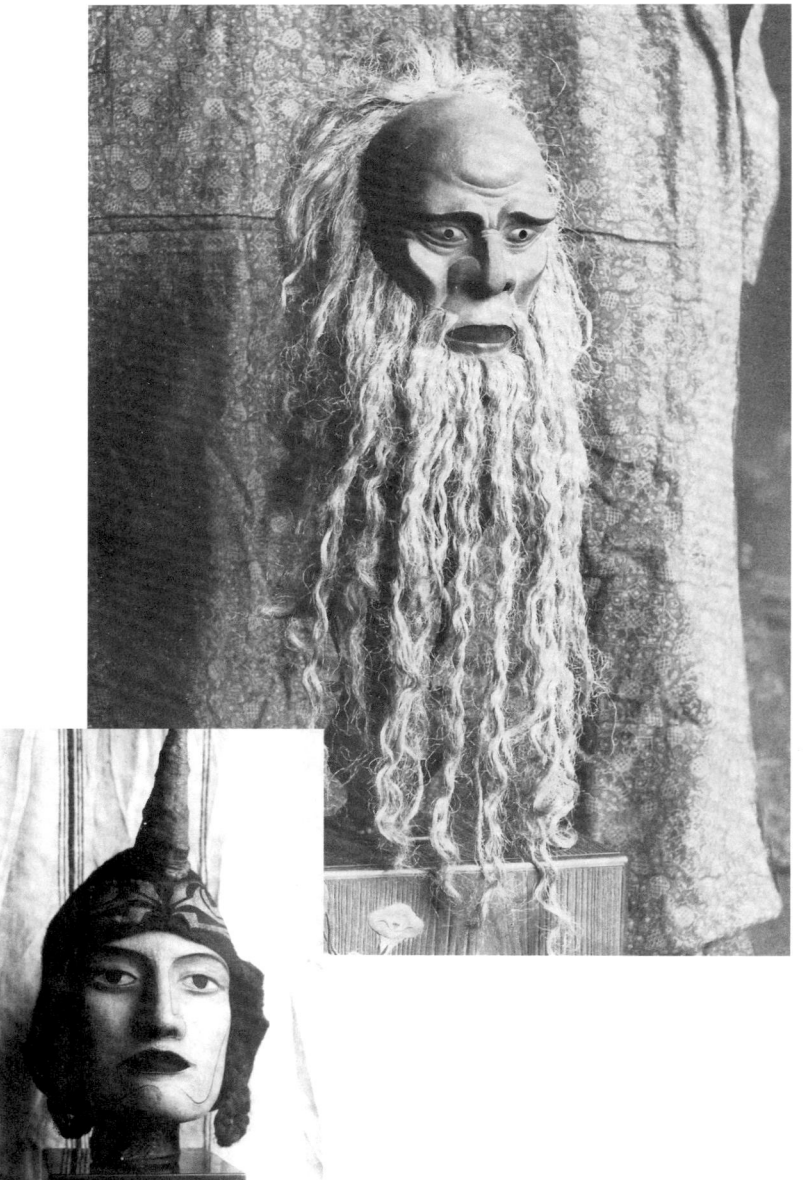

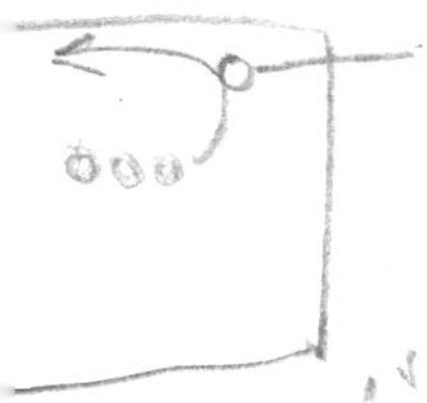

fig. 7

(They now go to one side of the stage, rolling up the cloth. A girl has taken her place by a square blue cloth representing a well. She is motionless.)

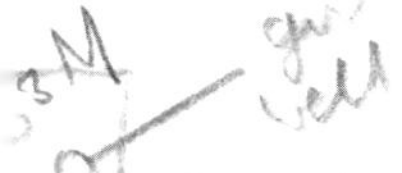

FIRST MUSICIAN.

Night falls.
The mountain-side grows dark,
The withered leaves of the hazel
Half choke the dry bed of the well.
The guardian of the well is sitting
Upon the old gray stone at its side,
Worn-out from raking its dry bed,
Worn-out from gathering up the leaves,
~~Her head is bowed,~~ her heavy eyes
Know nothing, or but look upon stone.
The wind that blows out of the sea
Turns over the heaped-up leaves at her side.
They rustle and diminish.

SECOND MUSICIAN.

I am afraid of this place.

BOTH MUSICIANS (singing)

"I alone cannot sleep," the heart cries,
"And the wind, the salt wind, the sea wind,"
"We alone under the skies,"
"We alone being blind."

FIRST MUSICIAN (speaking)

That old man climbs up hither
Who has been watching by this well
These fifty years,
He is all doubled up with age.
The old thorn-trees are doubled so
Among the rocks where he is climbing.

> (An old man ENTERS through the audience from
> the other side, he crouches down a little
> way from the well, moving his hands as if
> he were making a fire. He has, however,
> nothing in his hands.)

FIRST MUSICIAN (speaking)

He has made a little heap of leaves
He lays the dry sticks on the leaves.
And shivering with cold he has taken up
The fire-stick and socket from its hole.
He whirls it round to get a flame,
And now the dry sticks take the fire,
And now the fire leaps up and shines
Upon the hazels and the empty well.

MUSICIANS (singing)

"O wind, O wind, O sea-wind
"Let me sleep," cry the gray rocks of the steep,
"Let me sleep," cries the heart to the mind,
"I am old and would sleep."

fig. 9

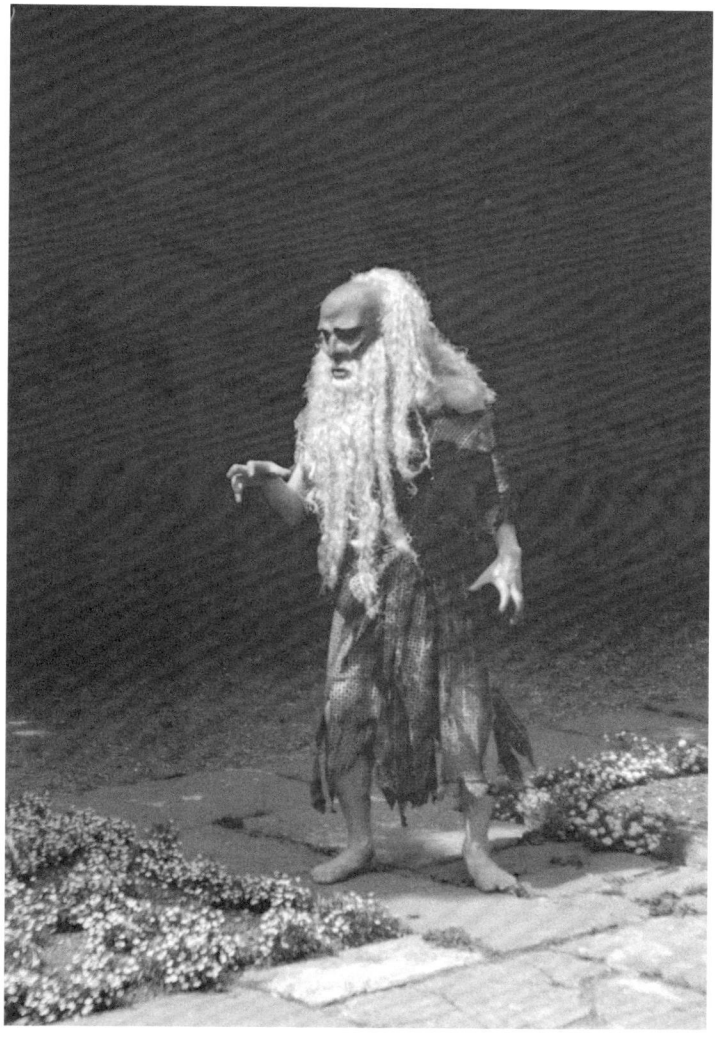

fig. 10

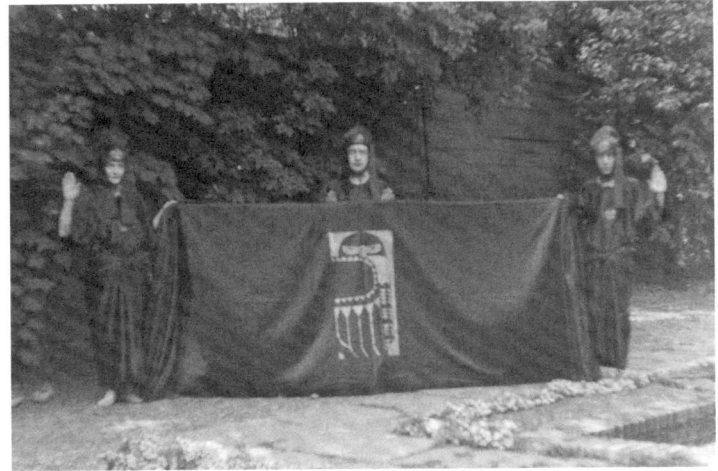

fig. 11

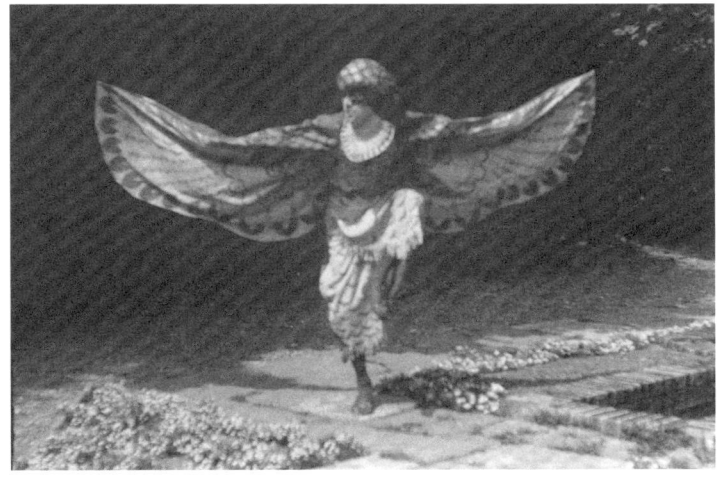

fig. 12

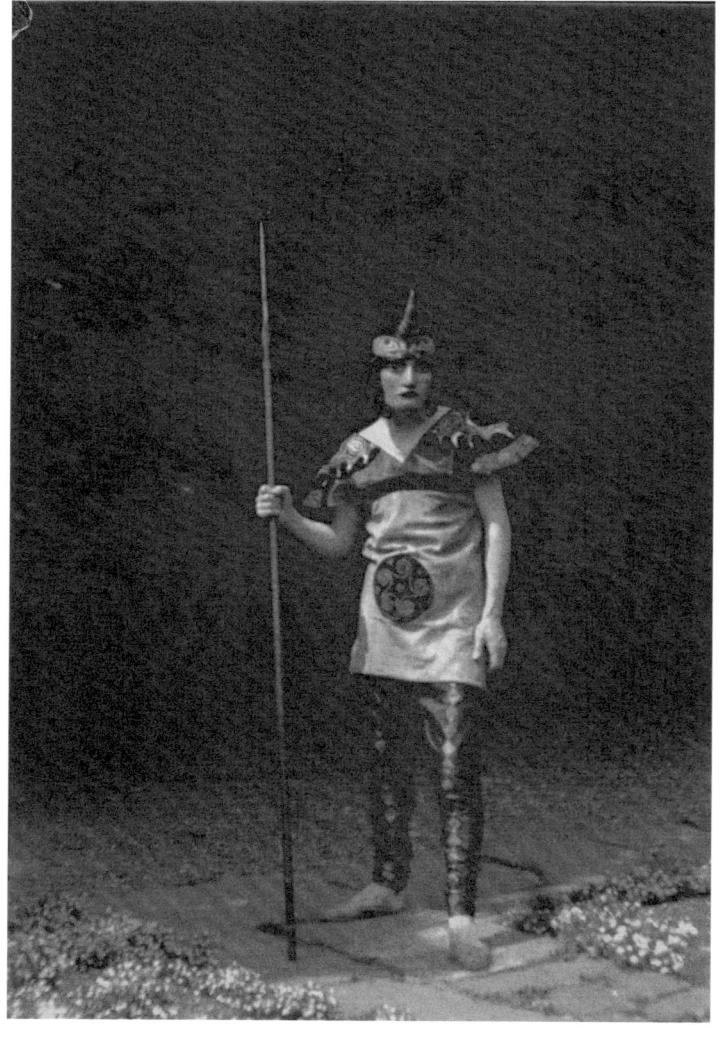

Yukie Kamiya, Director, The Japan Society Gallery

NOH REINCARNATED
'At Twilight' and the inspiration of Japanese Noh drama

One hundred years ago the year 1916 marked not only the birth of Dadaism in Zürich, but also the emergence of key works that would bring the traditional Japanese Noh play to widespread attention in the West and in particular the Anglosphere. One was the publication of a book of Noh plays in English translation by two Americans: Ernest Fenollosa (1853–1908), whose footprints as a scholar of Japanese art remain firmly imprinted on Japan and the United States today, and Ezra Pound (1885–1972) then a rising talent in poetry. Another was the inaugural performance in London of *At the Hawk's Well*, the first Noh-influenced dance play written by the great Irish poet W. B. Yeats (1865–1939), who was introduced to Noh as literature by Pound. Simon Starling's project *At Twilight* focuses on this moment when a rare blending of East and West, tradition and avant-garde, was forged by a diverse group of artists—escapees, largely, from the war—torn continent—through a series of coincidental encounters with Noh.

As a Noh-inspired play by a towering figure of modernist literature, *At the Hawk's Well* has repeatedly garnered attention not only in the West but in Japan as well. Yeats, who never saw a Noh performance, or even visited Japan, learned about this traditional Japanese masked dramatic form from Pound. Pound himself had begun work on English versions of Noh dramas without any understanding of traditional Noh plays or the Japanese language. It was Fenollosa who inspired Pound's enthusiasm for Noh.

Fenollosa was invited to Japan as a professor in philosophy and political economy, just as the country was emerging from its isolation of the mid-seventeenth to the mid-nineteenth centuries and engaging in a rapid about-turn to embrace Western culture and modernisation. He spent a total of seventeen years in Japan between 1878 and 1901, when he learned Noh songs and studied Noh drama under Minoru Umewaka, grand master of Noh. However, Fenollosa died in 1908 while in London conducting research at the British Museum. His widow Mary, who had been his assistant when he was Curator of Oriental Art at the Museum of Fine Arts, Boston, entrusted his sixteen notebooks containing translations of Japanese and Chinese literature as well as his manuscripts of Noh songs to Pound. While working as Yeats' secretary, and with editing assistance from various individuals including Arthur Waley, Pound published a book of fifteen Noh pieces in 1916, crediting Fenollosa as a co-translator. Through Pound, Yeats quickly came to understand the essence of Noh, and to be seduced by its world, which he connected at a fundamental level with Irish myth.

In the early phases of his project, Starling began by recreating the masks and costumes of characters in Yeats' drama—the Hawk, Old Man, Cuchulain—based on a few black and white photographs taken at the home of Lady Cunard (a shipping line heiress) during the first staging of *At the Hawk's Well* in April 1916. He went on to examine the complex intermingling of relationships between those involved in Yeats' play, blending historical facts with his own imaginative interpretations to embark on an ambitious piece of theatre with an original script depicting the human drama intimately linked to Yeats' drama.

fig. 13

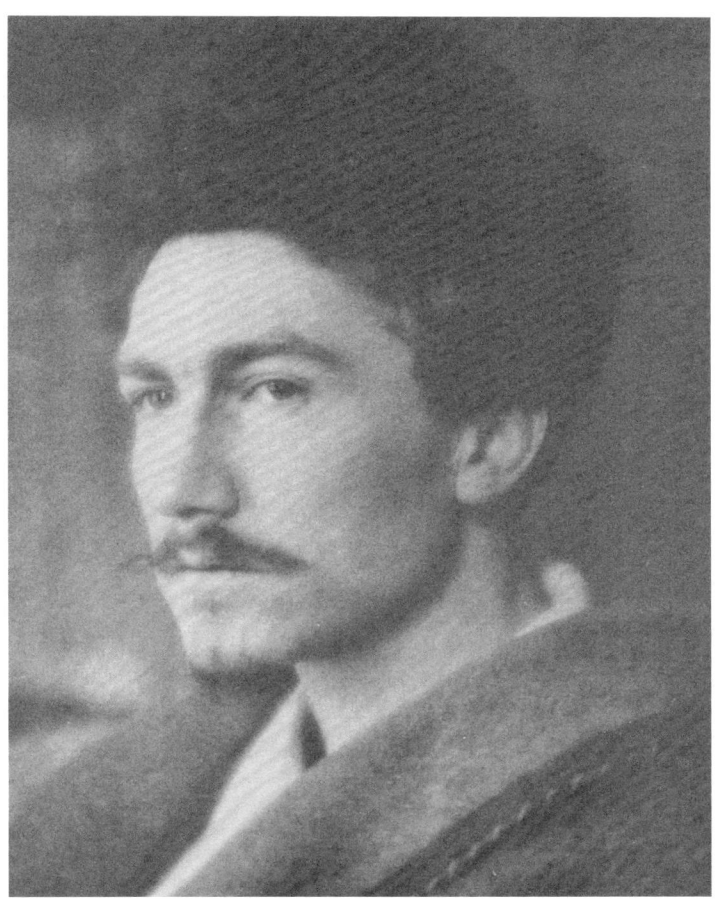

It should be remembered that *At the Hawk's Well*, was, in the course of time, imported back into Japan, the home of Noh, where it reinvigorated interest in to Noh itself. As early as 1920 the play was translated into Japanese by Tokuboku Hirata, a scholar of English literature, who was Fenollosa's assistant during his study of Noh. This was followed by several further translations over the years. The play was first performed in Japan in December 1939 in a Tokyo production marking the homecoming of Michio Ito, who had danced the part of the Hawk in 1916 and on this occasion, the Old Man.

Doubtless Yeats' play was viewed in Japan as a little odd to bear the appellation of Noh. However, in 1949, Noh scholar and theatre director Mario Yokomichi reworked the play to create a new Noh piece titled *Taka no Izumi* (The Hawk's Spring), first staged by Minoru Kita. In 1967, Yokomichi made further modifications to the play, radically reconfiguring and rewriting it as *Takahime* (The Hawk Princess). In 1990, the poet Mutsuo Takahashi developed the play into *Taka-no-i* (The Hawk's Well), making a total of three reworkings of the piece. Thus the impact of Noh on Western literature and theatre has come full circle, acting as a stimulus to Noh itself.

Noh is an ancient form of musical theatre first perfected by father and son Kan'ami and Zeami in the fourteenth century. It continued to be performed as a form of ritual under the patronage of generations of *shogun*. Thus this classical theatre form was preserved over several centuries. However, with the social and political changes that occurred in Japan the latter half of the nineteenth century, during the country's rapid drive toward modernisation, many classical art forms fell into decline and lost their patronage, including Noh. The artistic heritage of Japan was further threatened by the movement to abolish Buddhism and a burgeoning fashion of Westernisation. At the same time, enthusiasm for Japanese classical traditions was growing increasingly strong among Westerners, as typified by Fenollosa, and this in turn triggered a reappraisal of Japanese traditional art within Japan. Such reappraisal is exemplified by Michio Ito, who previously considered Noh to be tedious, but was awakened to it through the interest

fig. 14

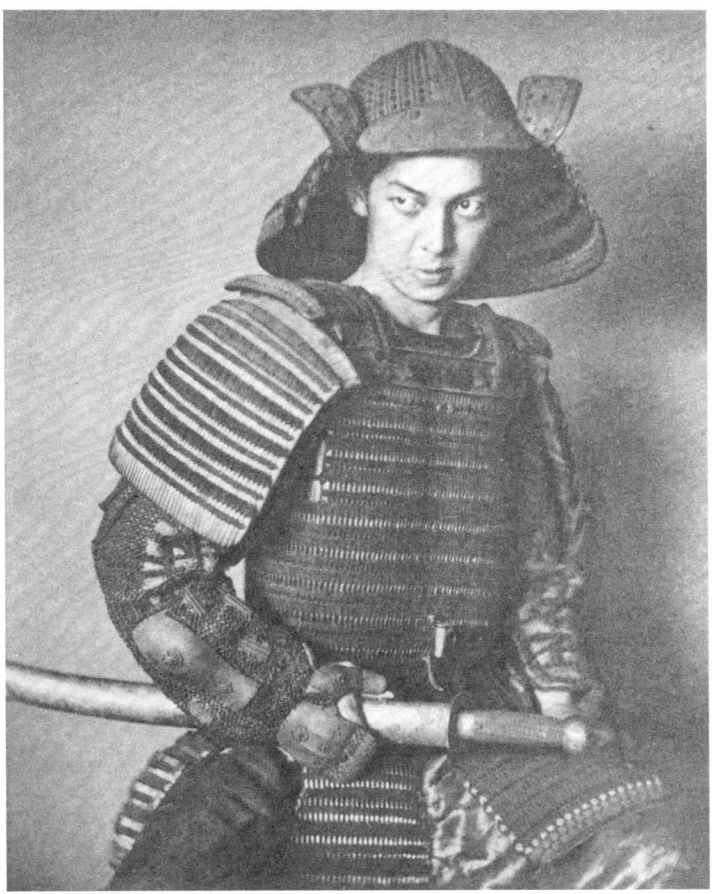

shown by Pound and Yeats, and ultimately became a major figure in its resurgence. Starling's project is another attempt to draw attention to the allure of Noh, in the vein of Pound and Yeats.

Starling first dealt with Noh in his work *Project for a Masquerade (Hiroshima)* (2010) which took a Cold War

fig. 15

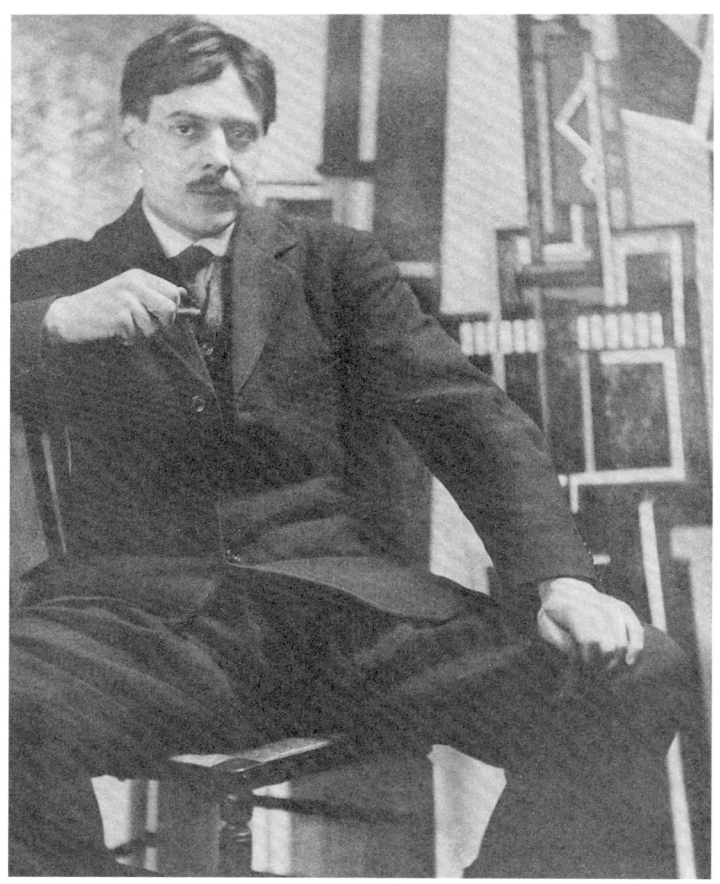

fig. 16

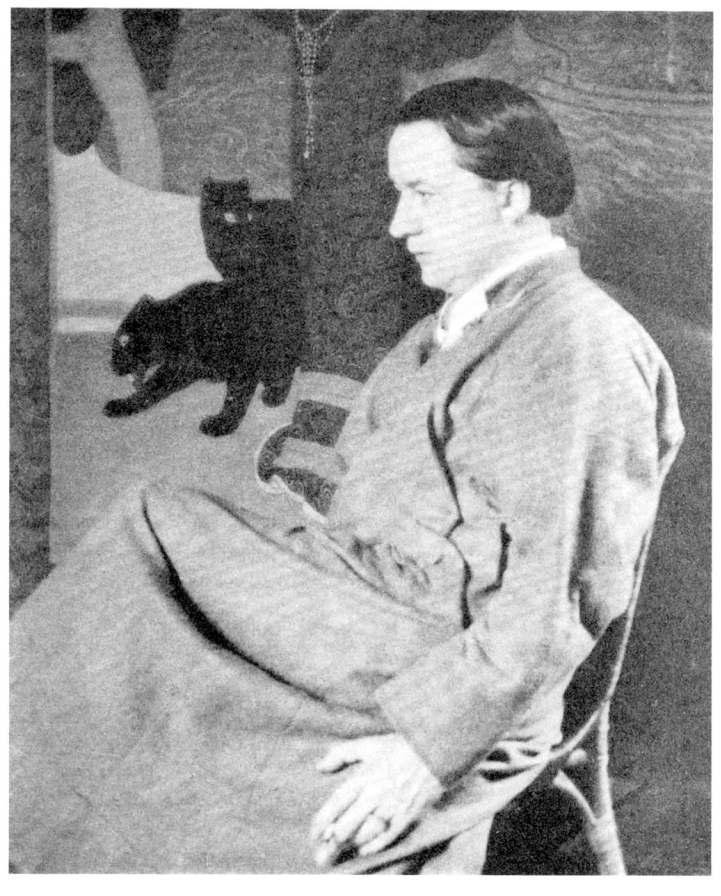

story about the great British sculptor Henry Moore, and reconfigured it based on *Eboshi-ori*, translated in *The Nō plays of Japan* (1921) by Arthur Waley, among the audience at the first performance of *At the Hawk's Well*. In the compact studio of Noh mask maker, Yasuo Miichi, in Osaka, newly-made masks of historical and fictional Cold War-era figures emerged from single blocks of wood. By collaborating with someone possessing the rare traditional skill of mask-making, Starling linked past and present to expose and spin a single tale.

French playwright and diplomat Paul Claudel (1868–1955), who was the brother of Camille Claudel and lived in Japan from 1921 to 1927, noted, "In drama, something happens; in Noh, somebody arrives." In Noh, where past and present, reality and illusion, share the same stage, all kinds of people appear from the past and present, reality and fantasy. For Starling, *At the Hawk's Well* represents a fusion of Western drama and Japanese traditional theatre where the seeds of a new kind of creative practice were sown. Through the project *At Twilight*, he has adopted the perspective to appreciate different cultures and used his distinctive powers of imagination to connect the various people involved in Yeats' creation, inviting them to appear.

The miraculous series of encounters with Noh, transmitted and re-transmitted across the sea, opened a platform for people working passionately toward understanding to direct respect and interest toward a culture created by others. Through their rich imaginations, they have filled in gaps where experience or information was lacking, at times causing misunderstanding, but ultimately leading to unexpected creativity in the repeated reincarnations of Noh. Like Yeats' creation one hundred years ago, Starling's genre-defying collaborative effort with expert practitioners in other fields invites the imagination to take flight from historical fact.

fig. 17

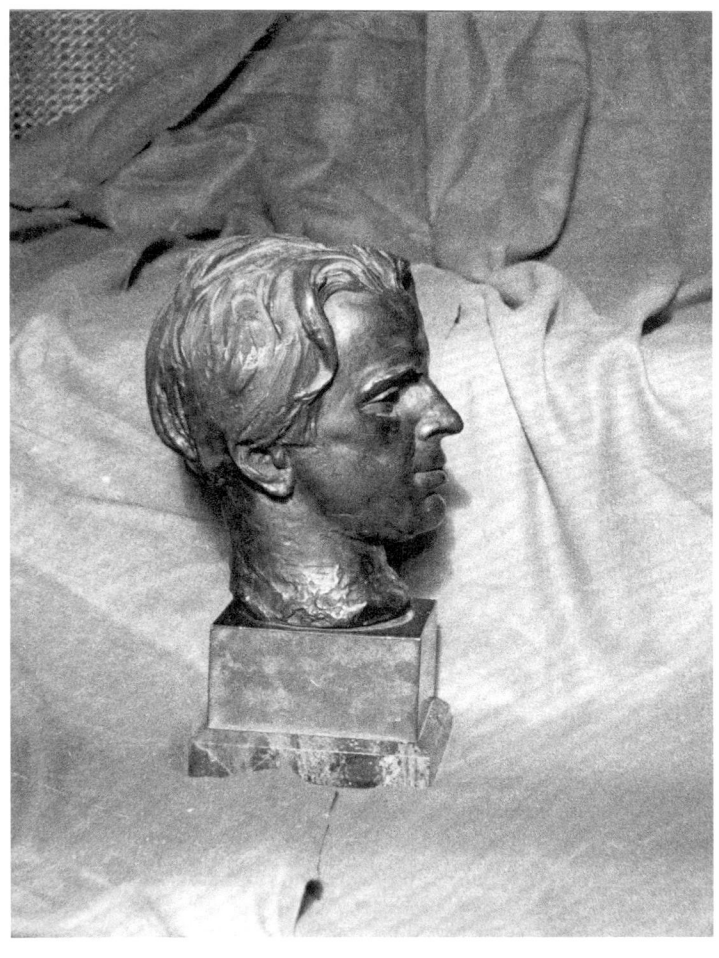

fig. 18

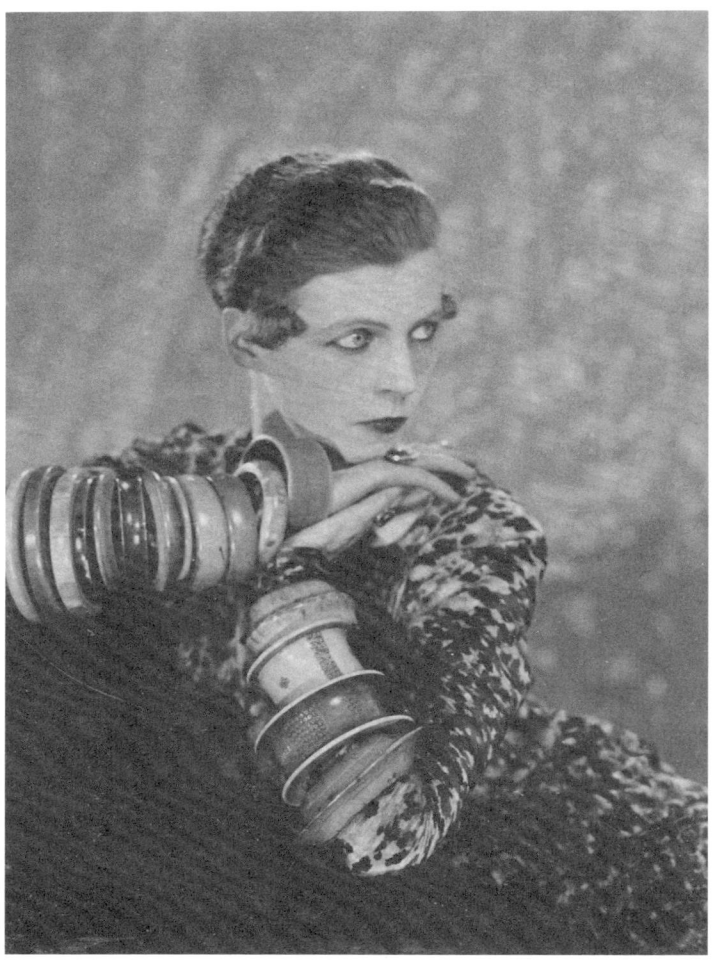

fig. 19

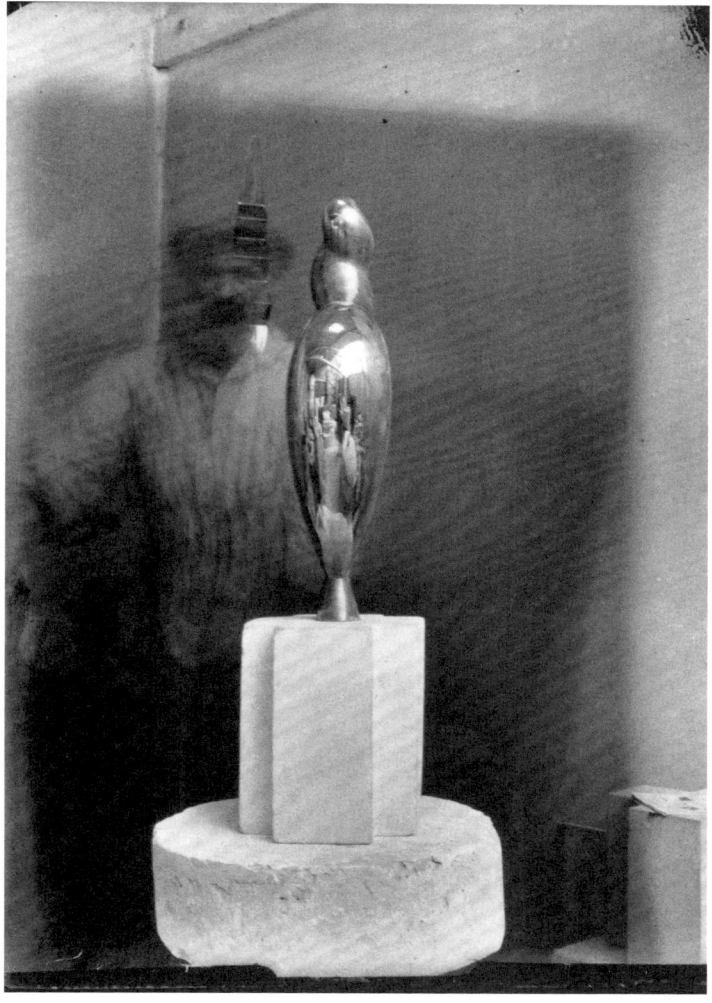

fig. 20

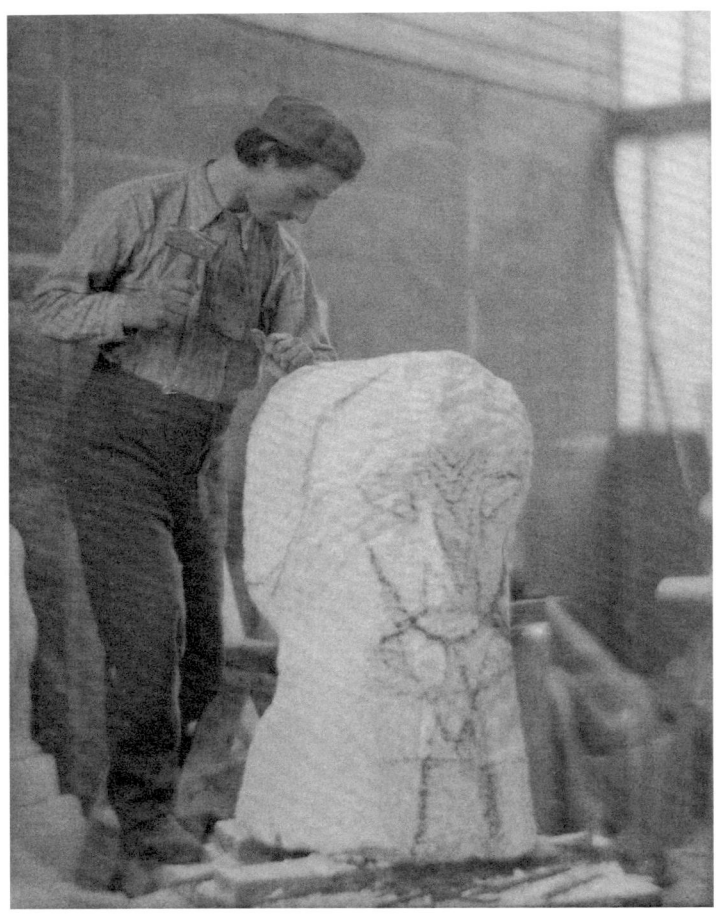

fig. 21

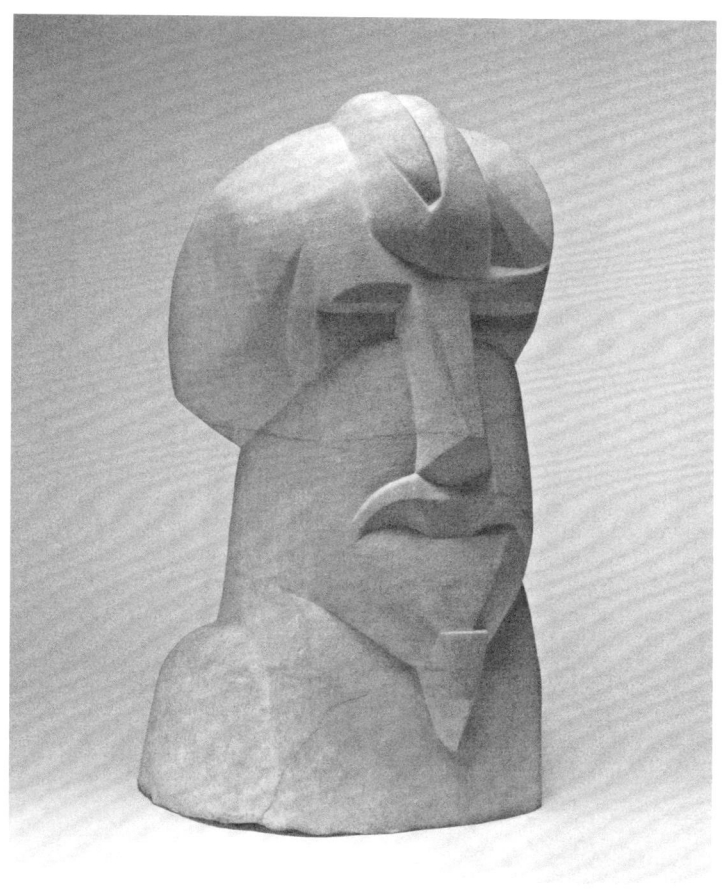

fig. 22

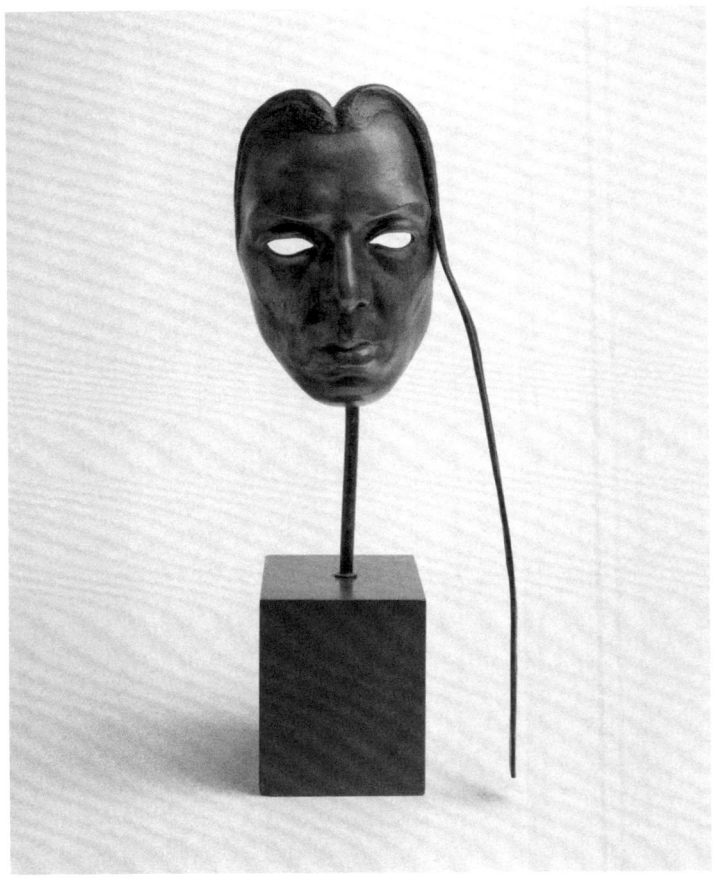

fig. 23

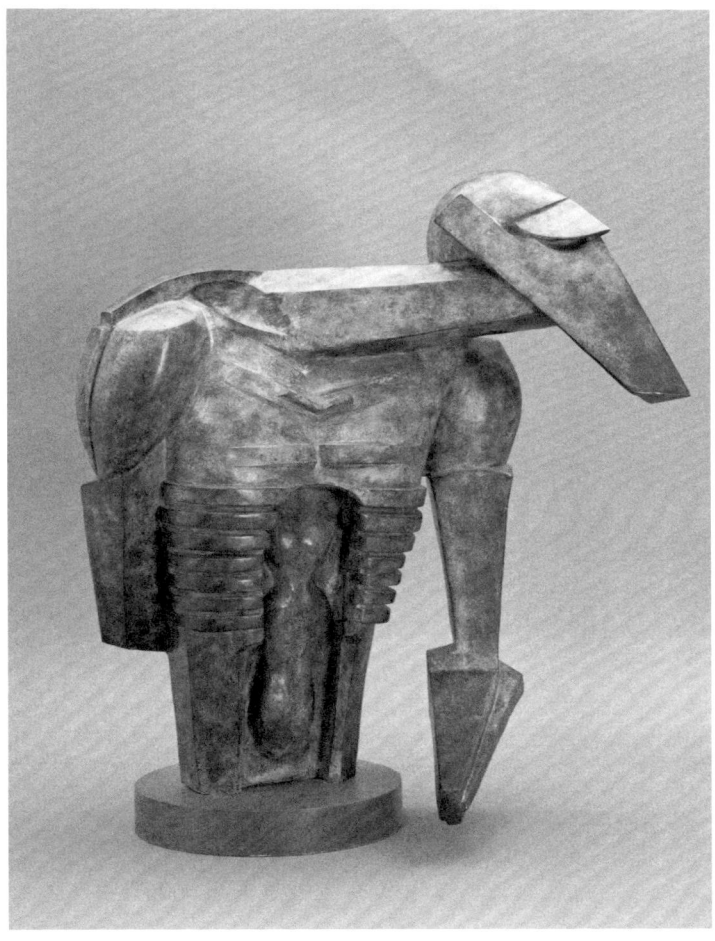

fig. 24

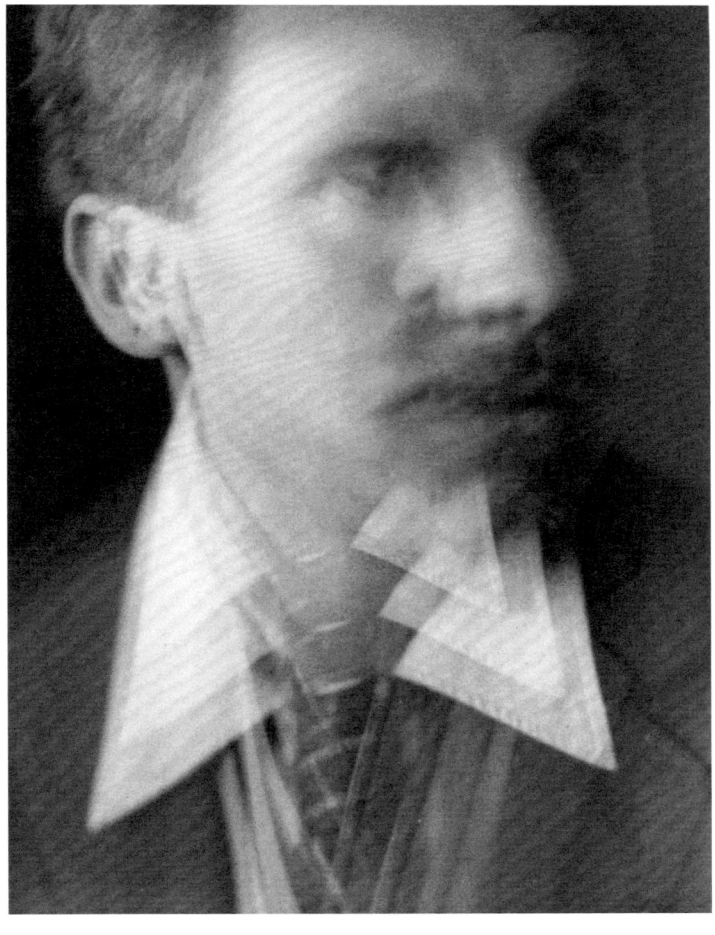

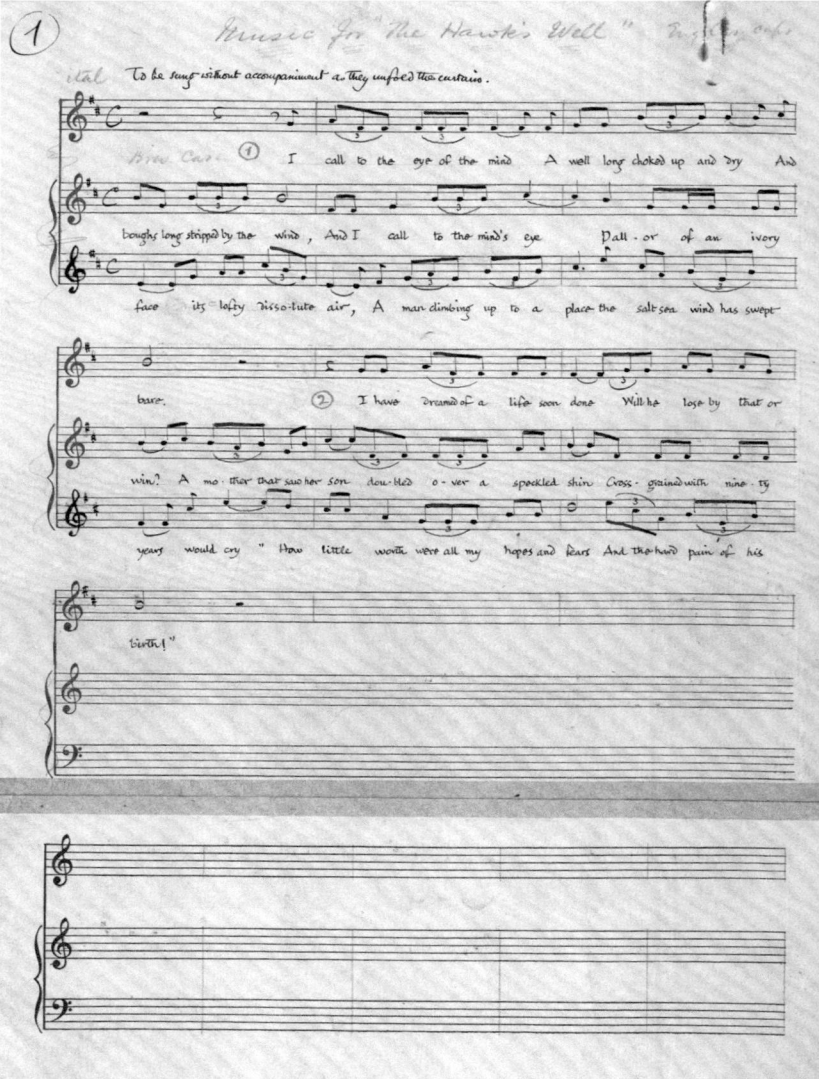

fig. 25

INVENTORY OF ASSOCIATED WORKS

Alvin Langdon Coburn (1882–1966)
Alvin Langdon Coburn, 1922
Photogravure from the book
More Men of Mark (1922)
Courtesy of Simon Starling

fig 16.
Alvin Langdon Coburn (1882–1966)
Edmund Dulac, 1914
Photogravure from the book
More Men of Mark (1922)
Courtesy of Simon Starling

fig 24.
Alvin Langdon Coburn (1882–1966)
Ezra Pound, 1916, printed ca. 1950
Gelatin silver print
Image courtesy of the George Eastman Museum, bequest of the photographer

fig 13.
Alvin Langdon Coburn (1882–1966)
Ezra Pound, 1913
Photogravure from the book
More Men of Mark (1922)
Courtesy of Simon Starling

Alvin Langdon Coburn (1882–1966)
H. H. Asquith, 1914
Photogravure from the book
More Men of Mark (1922)
Courtesy of Simon Starling

Alvin Langdon Coburn (1882–1966)
Jacob Epstein, 1914
Photogravure from the book
More Men of Mark (1922)
Courtesy of Simon Starling

fig 14.
Alvin Langdon Coburn (1882–1966)
Micha Itow [Michio Ito], 1915
Photogravure from the book
More Men of Mark (1922)
Courtesy of Simon Starling

Alvin Langdon Coburn (1882–1966)
Michio Ito Wearing Hawk Costume from W. B. Yeats' Play At the Hawk's Well, c. 1916, printed later
Gelatin silver print
George Eastman Museum, bequest of the photographer

fig 15.
Alvin Langdon Coburn (1882–1966)
Wyndham Lewis, 1916
Photogravure from the book
More Men of Mark (1922)
Courtesy of Simon Starling

Alvin Langdon Coburn (1882–1966)
W. B. Yeats, 1913
Digital print reproduced from the book
Men of Mark (1913)
The New York Public Library

Alvin Langdon Coburn (1882–1966)
Yone Noguchi, 1913
Photogravure from the book
More Men of Mark (1922)
Courtesy of Simon Starling

fig 19.
Constantin Brancusi (1876–1957)
Jeune Fille Sophistiquée, or *Portrait de Nancy Cunard*, 1928
Polished bronze, edition cast by Susse Fondeur, 2013
Estate of Constantin Brancusi, courtesy Paul Kasmin Gallery, NY

Dorothy Shakespear Pound (1886–1973)
Composition in Blue and Black, c. 1914–1915
Watercolor and collage on paper
Collection of the Ruth and Elmer Wellin Museum of Art at Hamilton College, Gift of Omar S. Pound, Class of 1951

INVENTORY OF ASSOCIATED WORKS

Dorothy Shakespear Pound (1886–1973)
Untitled, c. 1915–1920
Watercolor and graphite on wove paper
Collection of the Ruth and Elmer Wellin Museum of Art at Hamilton College, Gift of Omar S. Pound, Class of 1951

Ernest Fenollosa (1853–1908)
Certain Noble Plays of Japan, 1916
Book
Collection of Pratt Institute Libraries

Ezra Pound (1885–1972)
For Isamu Noguchi in Memory of Brancusi + Michio Ito, 1971
Ink on paper
The Isamu Noguchi Foundation and Garden Museum

Henri Gaudier-Brzeska (1891–1915)
Birds Erect, 1914
Limestone
The Museum of Modern Art, New York, Gift of Mrs. W. Murray Crane, 1945

Henri Gaudier-Brzeska (1891–1915)
Self-portrait Caricature, undated
Ink on paper
The San Diego Museum of Art, Gift of Mrs. Irving T. Snyder

fig 22.
Isamu Noguchi (1904 - 1988)
Michio Ito, 1925-1926
Bronze
Photo by Kevin Noble
The Isamu Noguchi Foundation and Garden Museum, New York / ARS

fig 23.
Jacob Epstein (1880-1959)
Rock Drill, 1913-1914
Bronze (cast 1962).
28 x 26", on wooden base 12" diam.
Mrs. Solomon Guggenheim Fund. (155.1962)
Digital Image © The Museum of Modern Art / Licensed by SCALA / Art Resource, NY

Jacob Epstein
Study for *Rock Drill*, c. 1913
Pencil on paper
The Museum of Modern Art, New York, Gift of Constance B. Cartwright, 1976

Jacob Epstein (1880–1959)
Study for *Rock Drill*, c. 1913
Chalk on paper
The Museum of Modern Art, New York, The Joan and Lester Avnet Collection, 1978

Jiro Nan'e (1902–1952)
Noh no Tenkai (The Evolution of Noh), 1954
Book
Private collection

Tsukioka Kōgyo (1869 – 1927)
Nōgaku Zue Vol. I, 1898–1899
Woodblock printed book (*orihon*, accordion-style); ink and color on paper
Private collection

Tsukioka Kōgyo (1869 – 1927)
Nōgaku Zue Vol. II, 1898–1899
Woodblock printed book (*orihon*, accordion-style); ink and color on paper
Private collection

Tsukioka Kōgyo (1869 – 1927)
Nōgaku Zue Vol. III, 1898–1899
Woodblock printed book (*orihon*, accordion-style); ink and color on paper
Private collection

Tsukioka Kōgyo (1869 – 1927)
Nōgaku Zue Vol. IV, 1898–1899
Woodblock printed book (*orihon*, accordion-style); ink and color on paper
Private collection

Tsukioka Kōgyo (1869 – 1927)
Nōgaku Zue Vol. V, 1898–1899
Woodblock printed book (*orihon*, accordion-style); ink and color on paper
Private collection

INVENTORY OF ASSOCIATED WORKS

Tsukioka Kōgyo (1869–1927)
Nōgaku Hyakuban, 1922–1926
Woodblock printed book (*orihon*, accordion-style); ink and color on paper
Courtesy of Ronin Gallery

Tsukioka Kōgyo (1869 – 1927)
Nōga Taikan, c. 1925–1930
Unbound collection of woodblock prints; ink and color on paper
Courtesy of Ronin Gallery

Tsukioka Yoshitoshi (1839 – 1892)
Kumasaka in the Misty Moonlight, undated
Polychrome woodblock print from the *One Hundred Aspects of the Moon* series (1885–1892)
Private collection

Deme Genkyū (Artist's Seal)
Noh Mask: Sankōjō, late 17th to mid-18th century
Wood, *gofun*, vegetable and mineral pigments, horse hair
Private collection

Unknown Artist
Noh Mask: Heita, Edo period
Wood, *gofun*, vegetable and mineral pigments
Private collection

Unknown Artist
Noh Mask: Shakumi, Muromachi period
Wood, *gofun*, vegetable and mineral pigments
Private collection

Attributed to Fukurai
Noh Mask: Zō-Onna, late 16th or early 17th century
Wood, *gofun*, vegetable and mineral pigments
Private collection

Unknown Artist
Noh Mask: Chūjō, Edo period
Wood, *gofun*, vegetable and mineral pigments
Private collection

Unknown Artist
Noh Mask: Yase Otoko, Edo period
Wood, *gofun*, vegetable and mineral pigments
Private collection

Unknown Artist
Noh Mask: Ko-Beshimi, mid-17th to early 18th century
Wood, *gofun*, vegetable and mineral pigments, gold
Private collection

Unknown Artist
Noh Mask: Uba, Muromachi period
Wood, *gofun*, vegetable and mineral pigments
Private collection

Unknown Photographer
Cenotaph for Ezra Pound with Henri Gaudier-Brzeska's Hieratic Head of Ezra Pound *(the 1914 original, or the authorized 1973 copy) on a platform designed by Isamu Noguchi, San Giorgio Maggiore, Venice*, c. 1974–1975 (two photographs)
Gelatin silver prints
The Isamu Noguchi Foundation and Garden Museum

Unknown Photographer
Nancy Cunard, 1916
Digital print
Harry Ransom Center, The University of Texas at Austin

Unknown Photographer
Photo of plaster study for Michio Ito, 1925
Gelatin silver print
The Isamu Noguchi Foundation and Garden Museum

INVENTORY OF ASSOCIATED WORKS

fig 20.
Walter Benington (1872-1936)
Henri Gaudier-Brzeska carving Hieratic Head of Ezra Pound, 1914
Gelatin silver print from the manuscript *A Life of Gaudier-Brzeska* by H. S. Ede (1929), Image courtesy of Leeds Museums & Galleries (Henry Moore Institute Archive)

William Butler Yeats (1865–1939)
Letter to Edmund Dulac, undated
Handwritten letter
Harry Ransom Center, The University of Texas at Austin

William Butler Yeats (1865–1939)
Letter to Edmund Dulac, March 23, 1916
Handwritten letter
Harry Ransom Center, The University of Texas at Austin

William Butler Yeats (1865–1939)
Letter to Edmund Dulac, February 13, 1916
Handwritten letter
Harry Ransom Center, The University of Texas at Austin

William Butler Yeats (1865–1939)
Letter to Edmund Dulac, March 5, 1916
Typewritten and signed letter
Harry Ransom Center, The University of Texas at Austin

William Butler Yeats (1865–1939)
Letter to Edmund Dulac, March 29, 1916
Handwritten letter
Harry Ransom Center, The University of Texas at Austin

William Butler Yeats (1865–1939)
Letter to Edmund Dulac, July 22, 1917
Handwritten letter
Harry Ransom Center, The University of Texas at Austin

William Butler Yeats (1865–1939)
Letter to Edmund Dulac, July 15, 1937
Typewritten letter
Harry Ransom Center, The University of Texas at Austin

Unknown Artist
Handwritten score for At the Hawk's Well
Music manuscript in pen
Harry Ransom Center, The Univerity of Texas at Austin

FURTHER ILLUSTRATIONS

fig. 1
The Guardian of the Well in
At the Hawk's Well, 1916
Frontispiece from the book *Four Plays for Dancers*, W.B. Yeats (The Macmillan Company, 1921)
Illustration/costume design by Edmund Dulac

fig. 2
Old Man in *At the Hawk's Well*, 1916
Page 9 from the book *Four Plays for Dancers*, W.B. Yeats (The Macmillan Company,1921)
Illustration/costume design by Edmund Dulac

fig. 3
Young Man in *At the Hawk's Well*, 1916
Page 15 from the book *Four Plays for Dancers*, W.B. Yeats (The Macmillan Company, 1921)
Illustration/costume design by Edmund Dulac

fig. 4
Edmund Dulac working on the masks for At the Hawk's Well, 1916
Image courtesy of Colin White

fig. 5
Edmund Dulac: Mask for Old Man, 1916
Image courtesy of Colin White

fig. 6
Edmund Dulac: Mask for Cuchulain, 1916
Image courtesy of Colin White

fig. 7
W.B. Yeats (1865–1939)
Original typewritten script for At the Hawk's Well *with handwritten annotations by W.B. Yeats and stage directions by Ezra Pound*, 1916
Image courtesy of Colin White

fig. 8
W.B. Yeats (1865–1939)
Original typewritten script for At the Hawk's Well *with handwritten annotations by W.B. Yeats and stage directions by Ezra Pound*, 1916
Image courtesy of Colin White

fig. 9
Alvin Langdon Coburn (1882–1966)
Allan Wade as the Old Man, 1916
Digital positive from unprinted negative, gelatin on nitrocellulose roll film
Image courtesy of the George Eastman Museum

fig. 10
Alvin Langdon Coburn (1882-1966)
The Three Musicians *from Yeats' play*, At the Hawk's Well, 1916. *(Edmund Dulac in center with the curtain he designed for the play)*, 1916
Digital positive from unprinted negative, gelatin on nitrocellulose roll film
Image courtesy of the George Eastman Museum

fig. 11
Alvin Langdon Coburn (1882-1966)
Michio Ito as The Hawk *in Yeats' Play* At the Hawk's Well, 1916
Digital positive of unprinted negative; gelatin on nitrocellulose roll film
Image courtesy of the George Eastman Museum

fig.12
Alvin Langdon Coburn (1882-1966)
British actor Henry Ainsley as Cuchulain *in Yeats' play*, At the Hawk's Well, 1916
Digital positive from unprinted negative, gelatin on nitrocellulose roll film
Image courtesy of the George Eastman Museum

FURTHER ILLUSTRATIONS

fig, 17
Bust of W. B. Yeats by Albert Power – photographed in profile, 1917
Image courtesy of UCD Digital Library from an original in UCD Special Collections.
© Professor Helen Solterer

fig. 18
Man Ray (1890–1976)
Nancy Cunard, 1926
Gelatin silver print
The Metropolitan Museum of Art, Ford Motor Company Collection, Gift of Ford Motor Company and John C. Waddell, 1987 (1987.100.131)
Image copyright © The Metropolitan Museum of Art. Image source: Art Resource, NY

fig. 19
Brancusi, Constantin (1876-1957)
Portrait of Nancy Cunard
Polished bronze (1928-1932), 1930
Photograph, glass negative with silver gelatine brome, 9.0 x 6.5 cm. PH361BIS.
Repro-photo: Bertrand Prévost
Musee National d'Art Moderne, Centre George Pompidou, Paris, France
© CNAC / MNAM / Dist. RMN-Grand Palais / Art Resource, NY
© Succession Brancusi - All rights reserved (ARS) 2016

fig. 21
Henri Gaudier-Brzeska (1891–1915)
Hieratic Head of Ezra Pound, 1914
© National Gallery of Art, Washington, DC

fig. 25
Edmund Dulac (1882–1953)
Original musical score for At the Hawk's Well, 1916
© Harry Ransom Center, The University of Texas at Austin

THE SCRIPT FOR AT TWILIGHT WAS PIECED TOGETHER FROM
A WIDE RANGE OF SOURCE MATERIAL THAT INCLUDED:

Beckett, Jane and Deborah Cherry: 'Reconceptualizing Vorticism: Women, Modernity, Modernism', in Paul Edwards (ed.), *Blast. Vorticism 1914-1918* (Burlington: Ashgate Publishing, 2000)

Caldwell, Helen: *Michio Ito. The Dancer and His Dances* (Berkeley: University of California Press, 1977)

Clark, David R. and Rosalind Clark: *W. B. Yeats & the Theatre of Desolate Reality* (Washington: The Catholic University of America Press, 1993)

Cork, Richard: *Vorticism and Abstract Art in the First Machine Age. Vol. 2. Synthesis and Decline* (London: Gordon Fraser, 1976) & *Wild Things. Epstein, Gaudier-Brzeska, Gill* (London: Royal Academy of Arts, 2009)

Ede, H. S.: *Savage Messiah. A biography of the sculptor Henri Gaudier-Brzeska* (Cambridge and Leeds: Kettle's Yard and Henry Moore Institute, 2011)

Fenollosa, Ernest and Ezra Pound: *The Noh Theatre of Japan. With complete Texts of 15 Classic Plays* (New York, Dover Publications, Inc., 2004)

Fleischer, Mary: *Embodied Texts: Symbolist Playwright-Dancer Collaborations* (Amsterdam and New York: Rodopi, 2007)

Gordon, Lois: *Nancy Cunard – Heiress, Muse, Political Idealist* (New York: Columbia University Press, 2007)

Ito, Michio: 'Omoide o Kataru: Takanoya [Memories of Things Past: Hawk's Well]', in *Hikaku Bunka, II* (Tokyo, 1956), pp. 57-76. (Helen Caldwell's transcription of recorded translation by Teizp Taya, 1974. From the UC Berkeley archives, E.A.L. 9215)

Kenny, Don: *A Guide to Kyogen* (Tokyo: Hinoki Shoten, 1998)

Lindsley, B.: 'W. B. Yeats' Encounters with His Daimon, Leo Africanus: The Daimon and Anti-Self Concepts in Per Amica Silentia Lunae' (Yeats Seminar, Fall 1995).

Longenbach, James: *Stone Cottage. Pound, Yeats & Modernism* (Oxford and New York: Oxford University Press, 1988)

Milne, A. A.: *Winnie-the-Pooh. The Original Version* (New York and Tokyo: Ishi Press, 2011)

Nadi, Aldo: *Nadi on Fencing* (New York: Dover Publications, Inc., 2005)

Noguchi, Yoné: *The Spirit of Japanese Poetry* (London: J. Murray, 1914)

Paige, D. D. (ed.): *The Letters of Ezra Pound 1907-1941* (London: Faber and Faber, 1951)

Pound, Ezra: *Gaudier-Brzeska. A Memoir* (New York: New Directions, 1974)

Somers, Emily Aoife: 'Transnational Necromancy', in Henrik Bogdan and Gordan Djurdjevic (ed.): *Occultism in a Global Perspective* (Durham: Acumen, 2013)

Tsukui, Nobuko: *Ezra Pound and Japanese Noh Plays* (Washington: University Press of America, 1983)

Wade, Allan (ed.): *The Letters of W. B. Yeats* (London: Rupert Hart-Davis, 1954)

Yeats, W. B.: *Four Plays for Dancers* (New York: The Macmillan Company, 1921)

Yeats, W. B.: *Selected Letters, 1915 – 1916*, The InteLex electronic edition of The Collected Letters of W. B. Yeats. Unpublished Letters (1905-1939)

Yeats, W. B.: 'The Poet and the Actress', in David R. Clark and Rosalind Clark: *W. B. Yeats & the Theatre of Desolate Reality* (Washington: The Catholic University of America Press, 1993)

COLOPHON

Published by The Common Guild, Dent-de-Leone, and Japan Society, New York on the occasion of the exhibitions

At Twilight
at The Common Guild
2 July – 4 September 2016

At Twilight (After W.B. Yeats' Noh Reincarnation)
at Japan Society, New York
14 October 2016 – 15 January 2017

and the first performances of
At Twilight: A play for two actors, three musicians, one dancer, eight masks (and a donkey costume)
Holmwood House, Glasgow
26, 27 and 28 August 2016

Editors: Kitty Anderson
and Simon Starling
Concept: Simon Starling
and Åbäke
Design: Åbäke
Printed by Die Keure, Belgium

All artworks © Simon Starling
Script © Graham Eatough and Simon Starling
All images courtesy of the artist and The Modern Institute, Andrew Hamilton/Toby Webster Ltd, Glasgow, unless otherwise stated
Texts © the authors
Publication © Simon Starling, The Common Guild, Dent-de-Leone, and Japan Society, New York.

All rights reserved. Apart from fair dealing for the purposes of private study, research, criticism or reviews as permitted under the Copyright Act, no part of this publication may be reproduced in any form without permission in writing from the publishers.

Every effort has been made to trace copyright holders and to obtain their permission for the use of copyright material. The publisher apologises for any errors or omissions and would be grateful if notified of any corrections that should be incorporated in future reprints or editions of this book.

ISBN 978—0—9558583—9—0
ISBN 978—1—907908—32—3
ISBN: 978—0—913304—04—4

Edition of 1650

The Common Guild
21 Woodlands Terrace
Glasgow, G3 6DF
UK
www.thecommonguild.org.uk

Dent-de-Leone
Black House
48 Wilton Way
London, E8 1BG
UK
www.dentdeleone.co.nz

Japan Society
333 East 47th Street
New York, NY 10017
www.japansociety.org

THANK YOU

Simon Starling would like to thank: Katrina Brown and her team at The Common Guild, Yukie Kamiya and her team at Japan Society, Maja McLaughlin and Karl Isakson at the studio, The Modern Institute, Glasgow, neugerriemschneider, Berlin, Casey Kaplan Gallery, New York and Galleria Franco Noero, Turin. Inspired by W.B. Yeats' 1916 production of *At the Hawk's Well*, *At Twilight* has been a deeply collaborative venture, only possible due to the extraordinary energy, skill and creative intelligence of all who worked on its realisation. It has been a huge privilege to work with them all. Special thanks must go to Graham Eatough who has been an irreplaceable and invigorating sparring partner throughout.

Graham Eatough would like to thank: Paddy Cuneen, Tomoko Komura, Gerry Mulgrew, Guy Coletta and Niall Black.

THE COMMON GUILD STAFF

Director: Katrina M. Brown
Curator: Kitty Anderson
Associate Producer: Katie Nicoll
Technical Manager: Stephen Murray
Programme Assistant: Brodie Sim
Finance Manager: Karen Vaughan
Admin Assistant: Elizabeth Hudson

The Common Guild is supported by Creative Scotland and Glasgow City Council.

At Twilight was commissioned by The Common Guild in collaboration with the Japan Society, New York and was supported by:

Creative Scotland
Outset Scotland
Sylvia Waddilove Foundation
Japan Society of the UK

With thanks to the National Trust for Scotland (especially all the staff at Holmwood House) and Scottish Ballet (especially Christopher Hampson, Hope Muir and Thomas Edwards).

Choreography by Javier De Frutos in association with Scottish Ballet
Music by Joshua Abrams and Natural Information Society
Costumes made in collaboration with Kumi Sakurai and Atelier Hinode Inc., Tokyo, Japan
Masks made in collaboration with Yasuo Miichi, Osaka, Japan
Blast tree made in collaboration with Simon Hopkins, Scott Associates Sculpture and Design, Glasgow with Alasdair Eckersall

All works courtesy of the artist and The Modern Institute, Andrew Hamilton/Toby Webster Ltd, Glasgow

THANK YOU

Simon Starling: *At Twilight (After W.B. Yeats' Noh Reincarnation)* at Japan Society is generously supported by Chris A. Wachenheim. Additional support is provided in part by New York City Department of Cultural Affairs in partnership with the City Council.

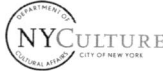

The exhibition at Japan Society is made possible in part by the Lila Wallace-Reader's Digest Endowment Fund, the Mary Griggs Burke Endowment Fund established by the Mary Livingston Griggs and Mary Griggs Burke Foundation, and Friends of the Gallery.

Arts & Culture Lecture Programs are made possible by funding from the Lila Wallace-Reader's Digest Endowment Fund. Additional support is provided by Chris A. Wachenheim and the Sandy Heck Lecture Fund.

LENDERS TO THE EXHIBITION

George Eastman Museum, New York
Harry Ransom Center, The University of Texas at Austin
Casey Kaplan Gallery, New York
Paul Kasmin Gallery, New York and the Estate of Constantin Brancusi
Leeds Museums and Galleries
The Museum of Modern Art, New York
The Noguchi Foundation and Sculpture Garden, New York
Ronin Gallery, New York
The San Diego Museum of Art
Scholten Gallery, New York
Ruth and Elmer Wellin Museum of Art, Clinton, NY
and Private collections

SPECIAL THANKS TO

Jenny Dixon
Chisa Fujiwara
Dakin Hart
David Libertson
Yasumasa Morimura
Katherine Martin
Aki Nagasaka
Roni Neuer
Mitsuko Ohno
Ariel Plotek
Allen Rosenbaum
Frederick Schultz
Hiroshi Sugimoto
Gensho Umewaka
Yokohama Triennial 2014

JAPAN SOCIETY STAFF

PRESIDENT
Motoatsu Sakurai

GALLERY
Director, Gallery: Yukie Kamiya
Curator of Exhibition Interpretation: Michael Chagnon
Exhibition Manager: Rylan Buchholz
Gallery Associate: Lia Monti
Gallery Interns: Neil Creveling Emily Furnival, Katherine Liang, and Xiaoyi Yang

DEVELOPMENT & EXTERNAL RELATIONS
Director, Foundation & Government: Ann Niehoff
Director, Corporate Giving: Yoko Suzuki
Director, Individual Giving: Kimberly Woodward
Director, Special Events: Christy Jones
Senior Development Officer: Mie Igarashi
Development Officer: Claudette Karabey
Development Associate: Lana Kitcher
Development Associate: Lydia Gulick

THANK YOU

MEDIA AND MARKETING
Director, Media & Marketing:
Michele Debreceni
Director, Communications:
Shannon Jowett
Web Producer: Nestor Martinez
Video Producer: Ben Warren
Press and Community Relations Officer:
Asako Sugiyama
Publications Manager: Cynthia Sternau
Manager of Graphic Design and
Productions: Malena Seldin

BOARD OF DIRECTORS
Jonathan E. Colby
Gerald L. Curtis
Richard A. Drucker
Louis J. Forster
Jacob A. Frenkel
Carol Gluck
Maurice R. Greenberg
Akira Harashima
Kevin T. Hogan
Yosuke Honjo
Ryota Isshiki
Joichi Ito
Jon C. Iwata
Merit E. Janow
Robert A. Karr
Frederick H. Katayama
Jonathan B. Kindred
Richard S. Lanier
Alan S. MacDonald
Jun Makihara
Yukihiko Matsumura
Kanetsugu Mike
Shinji Minobe
Hidemoto Mizuhara
Satoru Murase
Toby S. Myerson
Toshikazu Nambu
Fumio Otani
Joseph R. Perella
Punit Renjen
Justin A. Rockefeller
Wilbur L. Ross, Jr.
Motoatsu Sakurai

Takayuki Sawano
Timothy Schilt
Nicole Seligman
David Snoddy
Joshua N. Solomon Ed. D.
Hiroshi Suehiro
Reiichiro Takahashi
Yasushi Takahashi
Tsutomu Takemura
Gary M. Talarico
Chris Wachenheim
Tomofumi Yoshida
Susan J. Onuma

LIFE DIRECTORS
Deryck C. Maughan
Henry A. McKinnell, Jr.
Peter G. Peterson
Michael I. Sovern
Paul A. Volcker

(As of 1 May 2016)